THE
McKINSEY
WAY

Using the Techniques of the World's Top Strategic Consultants to Help You and Your Business

ETHAN M. RASIEL

McGraw-Hill

NEW YORK   SAN FRANCISCO   WASHINGTON, D.C.   AUCKLAND   BOGOTÁ
CARACAS   LISBON   LONDON   MADRID   MEXICO CITY   MILAN
MONTREAL   NEW DELHI   SAN JUAN   SINGAPORE
SYDNEY   TOKYO   TORONTO

Library of Congress Cataloging-in-Publication Data

Rasiel, Ethan M.
    The McKinsey way : using the techniques of the world's top strategic consultants
to help you and your business / Ethan M. Rasiel.
        p.   cm.
    Includes index.
    ISBN 0-07-053448-9
    1. McKinsey and Company. 2. Business consultants. 3. Industrial management.
I. Title.
    HD69.C6R38   1998
    658.4'012—dc21   98-51500
                                                                               CIP

McGraw-Hill

A Division of The McGraw-Hill Companies

4 5 6 7 8 9 0   DOC/DOC   9 0 4 3 2 1 0 9

ISBN 0-07-053448-9

The editing supervisor was Jane Palmieri,
the designer was Michael Mendelsohn, and
the production supervisor was Tina Cameron.
It was set in Sabon by MM Design 2000, Inc.

Printed and bound by R. R. Donnelley & Sons Company.

McGraw-Hill books are available at special quantity discounts to use
as premiums and sales promotions, or for use in corporate training
programs. For more information, please write to the Director of
Special Sales, McGraw-Hill, 11 West 19th Street, New York,
NY 10011. Or contact your local bookstore.

FOR
EMMA AND JESSICA

CONTENTS

ACKNOWLEDGMENTS ix

INTRODUCTION xi

PART ONE: THE McKINSEY WAY OF THINKING ABOUT BUSINESS PROBLEMS 1

1. Building the Solution 3
2. Developing an Approach 15
3. 80/20 and Other Rules to Live By 29

PART TWO: THE McKINSEY WAY OF WORKING TO SOLVE BUSINESS PROBLEMS 47

4. Selling a Study 49
5. Assembling a Team 57
6. Managing Hierarchy 65
7. Doing Research 71
8. Conducting Interviews 77
9. Brainstorming 93

PART THREE: THE McKINSEY WAY OF SELLING SOLUTIONS 103

10. Making Presentations 105
11. Displaying Data with Charts 113

12. Managing Internal Communications   119
13. Working with Clients   127

PART FOUR: SURVIVING AT McKINSEY   139

14. Find Your Own Mentor   141
15. Surviving on the Road   145
16. Take These Three Things with You Wherever You Go   149
17. A Good Assistant Is a Lifeline   153
18. Recruiting McKinsey Style   157
19. If You Want a Life, Lay Down Some Rules   163

PART FIVE: LIFE AFTER McKINSEY   167

20. The Most Valuable Lesson   169
21. Memories of McKinsey   175

INDEX   179

ACKNOWLEDGMENTS

I could not have written this book without the help, input, and support of many others. I would like to thank Julie Weed for getting the ball rolling and my agent, Daniel Greenberg, for keeping it in play. Thanks also to my editor, Mary Glenn, and all the team at McGraw-Hill Professional Book Group for believing in this project and helping make it a success. Much appreciation goes to Simon Carne, especially for his help with the section on MECE; many thanks as well to Adam Gold for pushing my thinking during the very early stages of this book. I thank my parents, Amram and Rosa Rasiel, for their understanding and assistance.

Of course, my deepest gratitude goes to those former McKinsey-ites who shared their knowledge and experiences with me. Without them, this book would never have come about. They are Kristin Asleson, Abe Bleiberg, Gresh Brebach, Tom Burke, Eric Hartz, Jason Klein, Hamish McDermott (you know who you are), Seth Radwell, Jeff Sakaguchi, Wesley Sand, Drew Smith, Suzanne Tosini, and the many others who, for their own reasons, did not wish their names mentioned.

INTRODUCTION

Think of this book as a sampler. You, the reader, need not start at the beginning and work your way through to the end. If you want to, feel free; otherwise, scan the table of contents and read whatever items interest you most.

ABOUT McKINSEY

To provide some background for those of you unfamiliar with McKinsey & Company, I offer a few words about the organization that its members past and present refer to as "the Firm." Since its founding in 1923, McKinsey & Co. has become the world's most successful strategic consulting firm. It currently has 75 offices (and counting) around the world and employs some 4500 professionals. It may not be the largest strategy firm in the world—some of the big accounting firms have larger practices—but it is certainly the most prestigious. McKinsey consults to most of the Fortune 100, as well as to many U.S. state and federal agencies and foreign governments. McKinsey is a brand name in international business circles.

Several senior McKinsey partners have risen to international prominence in their own right. Lowell Bryan advised the Senate Banking Committee during the savings and loan crisis. Kenichi Ohmae (who recently left the Firm) writes books on management and futurology that are best sellers in Japan. Herb Henzler advised former German Chancellor Helmut Kohl on business and economic matters. Even more visible are some of McKinsey's "alumni," who have gone on to senior positions around the world: Tom Peters, management guru and coauthor of *In Search of Excellence*; Harvey Golub, president of American Express; and Adair Turner, president of the Confederation of British Industries, to name but three.

To maintain its preeminent position (and to earn its high fees) the Firm seeks out the cream of each year's crop of business school graduates. It lures them with high salaries, the prospect of a rapid rise through McKinsey's meritocratic hierarchy, and the chance to mingle with the elite of the business world. In return, the Firm demands total devotion to client service, submission to a grueling schedule that can include weeks or months away from home and family, and only the highest-quality work. For those who meet McKinsey's standards, promotion can be rapid. Those who fall short soon find themselves at the latter end of the Firm's strict policy of "up or out."

Like any strong organization, the Firm has a powerful corporate culture based on shared values and common experiences. Every McKinsey-ite goes through the same rigorous training programs and suffers through the same long nights in the office. To outsiders, this can make the Firm seem monolithic and forbidding—one recent book on management consulting likened McKinsey to the Jesuits. In truth, as I hope this book will communicate, McKinsey is as human as its employees are.

The Firm has its own jargon too. It is full of acronyms: EM, ED, DCS, ITP, ELT, BPR, and so forth. McKinsey-ites call their assignments or projects "engagements." On an engagement, a McKinsey team will search for the "key drivers" in their quest to "add value." Like most jargon, much of this is simply verbal shorthand; some of it, however, once understood, can be as useful to business-people outside the Firm as it is to McKinsey-ites themselves.

In sum, like any powerful organization, McKinsey is complex. I hope this book will lift at least a corner of the veil of the McKinsey mystique and allow you, the reader, a peek into the inner workings of a very successful company.

ABOUT THIS BOOK

I have divided this book into five parts. In the first three, I explain how McKinsey-ites think about business problems and how they work at solving them. Parts One through Three are the "meat" of the book, and I hope that you will find in them something new to help you in your business career. In Part Four, I give some lessons McKinsey-ites have learned for coping with the stresses of life at the Firm. Anyone who works hard in today's business world should learn something useful—or at least amusing—there. Finally, Part Five briefly recounts some lessons learned at the Firm and shares a few memories of McKinsey.

I wrote this book with the goal of communicating new and useful skills to everyone who wants to be more efficient and effective in business. Anyone who wants to learn proven methods for approaching business problems in a structured, fact-based way will find them in these pages. And anyone looking for survival tips in the jungle of today's business world can benefit from doing things the McKinsey way.

In addition, this book will give any executive who works with management consultants, whether from McKinsey or elsewhere, some insight into how these strange beings think. Although each consulting firm has—or at least claims to have—its own methods, the root of all management consulting is the application of objective analysis by dispassionate outsiders. Other firms may not do things the McKinsey way, but their consultants' minds work in similar ways to McKinsey-ites'. Forewarned is forearmed.

I based this book on my own experience as a McKinsey associate from 1989 to 1992. I learned an enormous amount in that time, but scarcely enough for me to explain to the world the skills that McKinsey-ites use to succeed. Fortunately, I had help. I interviewed dozens of former associates, engagement managers, and partners of the Firm. Their knowledge and the lessons they learned during their time at McKinsey helped fill the many gaps in my own knowledge.

ABOUT CLIENTS

The word *client* appears in almost every chapter of this book. Since I'm writing from the McKinsey perspective, I use client to mean the organization for which you are solving a business problem. If you are not a consultant of some form, then strictly speaking, when you are working on a business problem, you don't have a client. I'd like to put it another way: You—or your organization—are your own client. Seen that way, the term *client* becomes applicable to any organization in which you work, whether as outsider or insider. In addition, I believe that thinking about your own organization as your client does make it easier to take advantage of the techniques in this book.

*   *   *

One of the cardinal virtues within McKinsey is confidentiality. The Firm guards its secrets closely. I, along with every other former McKinsey-ite, agreed never to disclose confidential information about the Firm and its clients, even after leaving McKinsey. I do not intend to break that agreement. Consequently, most of the names of companies and people in this book have been disguised.

As I said at the beginning, this book can be read from start to finish or dipped into like a box of chocolates. Whichever way you choose, I hope you'll find something you like.

THE
McKINSEY
WAY

THE McKINSEY WAY OF THINKING ABOUT BUSINESS PROBLEMS

McKinsey exists to solve business problems. The consultants who succeed at McKinsey *love* to solve problems. As one former EM* put it:

> Problem solving isn't a thing you do at McKinsey; it's what you do at McKinsey. It's almost as though you approached everything looking for ways it could be better, whatever it was. A part of you is always asking, "Why is something done this way? Is this the best way it can be done?" You have to be fundamentally skeptical about everything.

Part One describes *how* McKinsey thinks about business problems. It shows what it means to be fact-based, structured, and hypothesis-driven. It will tell you the McKinsey way to approach a business problem, and offer you a few choice rules to live by when trying to solve them.

---

*Engagement manager. The EM is in charge of the day-to-day work of a McKinsey team.

1

BUILDING THE SOLUTION

Like all things McKinsey, the Firm's problem-solving process has three major attributes. When team members meet for the first time to discuss their client's problem, they know that their solution will be

- Fact-based
- Rigidly structured
- Hypothesis-driven*

In this chapter, you will learn exactly what these attributes mean and how you can apply them in your business.

---

*At McKinsey, three is a magic number. Things at the Firm come in threes. Notice that this list has three items. Ask a McKinsey-ite a complex question, and you are likely to hear "There are three reasons. . ." Then, of course (as you will learn later in the book) there is the true McKinsey hierarchy for consultants—in descending order: client, Firm, you.

FACTS ARE FRIENDLY

Facts are the bricks with which you will lay a path to your solution and build pillars to support it. Don't fear the facts.

Problem solving at the Firm begins with facts. On the first day of an engagement, all members of the team comb through stacks of articles and internal research documents to gather enough facts to illuminate their piece of the problem for the first team meeting. Having drawn up an initial hypothesis for the problem, the team then races to gather the facts necessary (when put through the appropriate analyses) to support or refute it.

At the start of your time at McKinsey, gathering and analyzing facts is your raison d'étre. As one former SEM* observed:

> When you strip away a lot of the high-minded language with which McKinsey dresses up its problem-solving process, it comes down to very careful, high-quality analysis of the components of the problem combined with an aggressive attitude toward fact gathering.

Why are facts so important to the way McKinsey does business? There are two reasons. First, facts compensate for lack of gut instinct (see " . . . But Every Client Is Unique" in Chapter 2). Most McKinsey-ites are generalists. They know a little about a lot of things. As they gain experience and move through the ranks, they may come to know a lot about a lot of things. Even at this point, however, they will still know less about, say, inventory

---

*Senior engagement manager. In many ways a junior partner, the SEM is in charge of multiple studies and is expected to take a hand in client relations. SEMs get all the stress of partnership with less pay.

management practices for perishable foodstuffs than the folks who have been running the distribution operations of Stop & Shop for the last 10 years. Gut instinct might tell those folks the solution to an inventory management problem in 10 seconds (although they still would be wise to check the facts); McKinsey will go to the facts first.

Second, facts bridge the credibility gap. When she joins the Firm, the typical associate* (at least in the United States.) will have graduated near the top of her college class, spent two or three years working for a large company, then received her MBA from a top business school. She will be in her mid- to late twenties. On her first engagement she may have to present her analysis to the CEO of a Fortune 50 company, who will not give much credence to what some newly minted, 27-year-old MBA has to say—unless she has an overwhelming weight of facts to back her up. This is just as true for a junior executive presenting a proposal to his boss.

Despite (or possibly because of) the power of facts, many businesspeople fear them. Perhaps they are afraid that if they look too closely at the facts, they—or someone above them—might not like what they see. Maybe they think that if they don't look, the nasty facts will go away—but they won't. Hiding from the facts is a prescription for failure—eventually, truth will out. You must not fear the facts. Hunt for them, use them, but don't fear them.

---

*Associate: An entry-level McKinsey consultant, usually with an MBA. Technically, every consultant who has not made partner, even the hottest SEM, is still an associate of the Firm.

FEEL FREE TO BE MECE

To structure your thinking when solving business problems (or anything, for that matter), you must be complete while avoiding confusion and overlap.

MECE (pronounced "me-see") stands for "mutually exclusive, collectively exhaustive" and it is a sine qua non of the problem-solving process at McKinsey. MECE gets pounded into every new associate's head from the moment of entering the Firm. Every document (including internal memos), every presentation, every e-mail and voice mail produced by a McKinsey-ite is supposed to be MECE. Ask any number of McKinsey alumni what they remember most about the way the Firm solves problems and they will tell you, "MECE, MECE, MECE."

MECE structures your thinking with maximum clarity (hence minimum confusion) and maximum completeness. MECE starts at the top level of your solution—the list of issues making up the problem you have to solve. When you think you have determined the issues, take a hard look at them. Is each one a separate and distinct issue? If so, then your issue list is *mutually exclusive*. Does every aspect of the problem come under one (and only one) of these issues—that is, have you thought of everything? If so, then your issues are *collectively exhaustive*. Suppose your team is working on a study for that famous American manufacturing firm Acme Widgets. The problem you face is "We need to sell more widgets." Your team might come up with a list of the following ways to increase widget sales:

- Changing the way we sell our widgets to retail outlets.
- Improving the way we market our widgets to consumers.
- Reducing the unit cost of our widgets.

If this list looks rather generic, that's fine; we will talk about moving down a level of detail in the next section. What matters is that the list is MECE.

Suppose you add another item, say, "Reengineering our widget production process." How does that fit with the three issues you already have? This is certainly an important issue, but it isn't a fourth point alongside the others. It falls under "Reducing the unit cost," along with other subissues such as "Leveraging our distribution system" and "Improving our inventory management." Why? Because all these are ways to reduce the unit cost of widgets. Putting any (or all) of them with the other three issues on the list would cause an overlap. The items in the list would no longer be mutually exclusive. Overlap represents muddled thinking by the writer and leads to confusion for the reader.

Once you have a list in which all the items are separate and distinct (i.e., mutually exclusive), you have to check that it also includes every issue or item relevant to the problem (i.e., it is collectively exhaustive). Go back for a moment to "Reengineering our widget production process." You put this under "Reducing the unit cost." Now one of your team members says, "We should think about ways to improve widget quality through the production process."

She's right. Does this mean you should go back to having reengineering as an issue in its own right? No, but you should refine your list to include, under "Reducing unit cost," the subissue "Reengineering the production process to reduce unit cost," and, under "Improving the way we market . . . ," the subissue "Reengineering the production process to improve widget quality." Now you have something that looks like this:

- Changing the way we sell our widgets to retail outlets.
- Improving the way we market our widgets to consumers.

–Reengineering the production process to improve widget quality.
- Reducing the unit cost of our widgets.
–Reengineering the production process to reduce unit cost.

Suppose your team has come up with some interesting ideas that don't fit under the main issues. What then? You could ignore those points, but that wouldn't help Acme. You could make them issues in their own right, but then you would have too many issues. A good McKinsey issue list contains neither fewer than two nor more than five top-line issues (of course, three is best).

There is a solution to this dilemma—the magical category "Other Issues." If you can't figure out where to put those two or three brilliant ideas, there is always Other Issues. There is a caveat, however. Avoid using Other Issues in your top-line list—it looks out of place. It's fine lumped in among a bunch of subissues, but on the first slide of a big presentation, it sticks out. So try a little harder to fit those brilliant ideas into your top-line issues. Chances are you can. Still, if all else fails, Other Issues will help you stay MECE.

SOLVE THE PROBLEM AT THE FIRST MEETING—THE INITIAL HYPOTHESIS

Solving a complex problem is like embarking on a long journey. The initial hypothesis is your problem-solving map.

The initial hypothesis (IH), the third pillar of the McKinsey problem-solving process, is the most difficult to explain. To make the explanation easier for you (and me), I will break this section into three parts:

- Defining the initial hypothesis.
- Generating the initial hypothesis.
- Testing the initial hypothesis.

DEFINING THE INITIAL HYPOTHESIS

The essence of the initial hypothesis is "Figure out the solution to the problem before you start." This seems counterintuitive, yet you do it all the time.

Suppose you have to drive to a restaurant in a part of town you don't know. You know you have to make the third left off Smith Street and then take the first right; it's just after that corner. You know how to get to Smith Street; you'll just follow your directions from there. Congratulations, you have an initial hypothesis.

Solving business problems is more complicated than finding a restaurant, but the initial hypothesis works the same way. It is a road map, albeit hastily sketched, to take you from problem to solution. If your IH is correct, then solving the problem means filling in the details of the map through factual analysis.

Let's return to Acme Widgets from the last section. You and your team must find a way to increase sales at the widget business unit. After you've brainstormed using your knowledge of the widget business, but before you've spent a lot of time gathering and analyzing the facts, you might come up with the following top-line IH:

We can increase widget sales by:
- Changing the way we sell our widgets to retail outlets.
- Improving the way we market our widgets to consumers.
- Reducing the unit cost of our widgets.

As I will show in the next section, you would then take each issue down to another level or two of detail to determine which analyses you need in order to prove or disprove each hypothesis.

Remember that a hypothesis is merely a theory to be proved

or disproved. It is not the answer. If your IH is correct, then, a few months down the road, it will be the first slide in your presentation. If it turns out to be wrong, then, by proving it wrong, you will have enough information to move toward the right answer. By putting your IH down on paper, and determining how you can prove or disprove it, you have set up a road map that you can follow to an eventual proved solution.

GENERATING THE INITIAL HYPOTHESIS

The IH emerges from the combination of facts and structure. Therefore, as the first step in generating an IH, you must start with the facts. Remember, however, that you don't want to do a lot of digging around for information before you know *where* to dig. One former McKinsey SEM had a good approach for generating IHs:

> At the start of an engagement, I would just try to digest as much of our fact base as possible. I would sit down with the trade publications in that industry for an hour or two—not so much to gather facts as to absorb something of the flavor of that industry: what the jargon is, what the current industry issues are. I would especially seek out people in the Firm who knew about this particular industry. That was the quickest, most efficient way to get up to speed.

When generating an initial hypothesis, you don't need all the facts, just enough to have a good overview of the industry and the problem. If the problem is in your own business, you may already have the facts in your head. That's great, but facts are not enough. You have to apply structure to them.

To structure your IH begin by breaking the problem into its components—the key drivers (see "Find the Key Drivers," in Chapter 3). Next, make an *actionable* recommendation regarding each driver. This is extremely important. Suppose your business's profits are greatly affected by the weather; in fact, it is the key determinant of profits in a given quarter. "We have to pray for good weather" is not an actionable recommendation. On the other hand, "We must reduce our vulnerability to changes in the weather" is an actionable, top-line recommendation.

For your next step, you must take each top-line recommendation and break it down to the level of issues. If a given recommendation is correct, what issues does it raise? Consider the likely answers to each issue. Then go down another level. For each issue, what analyses would you need to make to prove or disprove your hypothesis? With a little experience, and a lot of debate within your team, you should get a good sense of what is provable and what is not. This will help you avoid blind alleys.

In the Acme Widgets problem, suppose your team decided that the key drivers were the sales force, the consumer marketing strategy, and production costs. You then came up with a list of actionable, top-line recommendations as your initial hypothesis:

We can increase widget sales by:
- Changing the way we sell our widgets to retail outlets.
- Improving the way we market our widgets to consumers.
- Reducing the unit cost of our widgets.

Let's begin with a closer look at the sales force. It's organized geographically (Northeast, Mid-Atlantic, Southeast, etc.) and sells primarily to three types of retail outlets: superstores, department stores, and specialty stores. The team believes that the sales force ought to be organized by customer type—that's one issue.

What analyses could prove or disprove that belief? You could break out the sales by customer type for each region. If penetration of superstores in the Northeast is higher than in any other region and higher than for the other types of retail outlets, find out why. When you talk to the Northeast sales reps, you might find that they have a better feel for superstores than any other sales team. What if they were put in charge of all superstores across the country and achieved the same penetration? What would that mean for widget sales?

The end product of this exercise is what McKinsey calls the *issue tree*. In other words, you start with your initial hypothesis and branch out at each issue. The result looks like the figure below.

When you've completed your issue tree, you have your problem-solving map. That's the easy part. The difficult part will come when you have to dig deep to prove your hypothesis.

ISSUE TREE FOR ACME WIDGETS

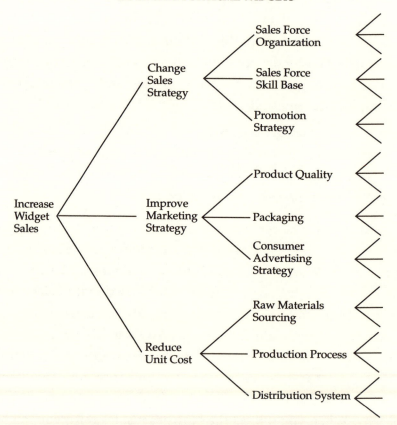

TESTING THE INITIAL HYPOTHESIS

Before you take your problem-solving map out on the road, you want (forgive the mixed metaphor) to kick the tires on it. Test it. Is it the best possible hypothesis you could devise, given what you know about the industry and your client or company? Have you thought about all the issues? Have you considered all the drivers of the problem? Are all your recommendations actionable and provable?

When I discussed generating an IH, I used the phrase "your team" rather than "you." My experience at the Firm (and that of the many McKinsey alumni I interviewed for this book) taught me that IHs produced by teams are much stronger than those produced by individuals. Why? Most of us are poor critics of our own thinking. We need others to pick apart our ideas. A team of three or four bright individuals is an excellent vehicle for that.

So when your team meets to come up with an IH let a thousand flowers bloom. Everyone should have his or her own ideas and initial hypotheses. Everyone should be prepared to push a teammate's thinking and test each new idea. If you are the team leader, you should try to be the thought leader too. Try to take a different approach from whatever has just been said. Ask, "What if we change this? What if we push that? How about looking at it this way?" The process involves shooting a certain amount of bull. That's OK, have fun—as long as it pushes your thinking. (For more ideas and techniques to push your team's thinking, see Chapter 9.)

2

DEVELOPING AN APPROACH

Just knowing the essence of the McKinsey problem-solving process does not mean you can now go forth and conquer the business world by being fact-based, structured, and hypothesis-driven. No two business problems are identical; you must figure out how to approach each problem in order to devise the best solution for it.

In this chapter, I will explain how McKinsey-ites approach business problems and apply the McKinsey problem-solving process to maximum effect.

THE PROBLEM IS NOT ALWAYS THE PROBLEM

Sometimes a business problem will land on your desk and you will be told to solve it. Fair enough. But before you go rushing off in any particular direction, make sure you're solving the right problem—it may not be the one you were given.

A McKinsey alumnus with a scientific background told me that business problem solving is organic and complex, like medicine. A patient will come into a doctor's office and say that he thinks he has the flu. He will tell the doctor about his symptoms: scratchy throat, achy head, and runny nose. The doctor will not immediately trust the patient's conclusion. She will take the patient's history, ask some probing questions, and then make her diagnosis. The patient may have the flu, or a cold, or something more serious, but the doctor will not rely on the patient to diagnose himself.

At McKinsey, we found that clients were often no better at diagnosing themselves than a doctor's patients. Sometimes, problems would come to us in extremely vague formulations. In my first study at the Firm, our team's mission was to help a New York investment bank "increase profitability"—the business equivalent of a patient telling the doctor "I don't feel well." In another case, a McKinsey team went in to evaluate expansion opportunities for a division of a manufacturing company. After a few weeks of gathering and analyzing data, the team realized that what the division needed was not expansion; it was closure or sell-off.

The only way to figure out if the problem you have been given is the real problem is to dig deeper. Get facts. Ask questions. Poke around. It usually does not take very long to figure out if you are heading down the right path, and the time you take up front will more than make up for itself in time you don't waste further down the line.

What do you do when you are convinced you are working on the wrong problem? When a doctor thinks that a patient's minor symptoms mask something more serious, she will tell her patient, "Mr. Jones, I can treat your headache, but I think it's a symptom of something more serious and I'd like to do further tests." In the same way, you should go back to your client, or your boss—whoever it was that asked for your input in the first place—and say, "You asked me to look at problem X, but the real impact on our performance will come from solving problem Y. Now I can solve problem X, if that's what you really want, but I think it's in our interest to focus on Y." If you have the data to back you up, the client can either accept your recommendation or tell you to stay on the original problem, but you will have fulfilled your responsibility to act in the client's best interests.

DON'T REINVENT THE WHEEL (PART 1)

Most business problems resemble each other more than they differ. This means that with a small number of problem-solving techniques, you can answer a broad range of questions. These techniques may be somewhere in your organization, either written down or in the heads of your fellow employees. If not, use your experience to develop your own tool kit.

McKinsey, like every other consulting firm, has developed a number of problem-solving methods and given them fancy names: Analysis of Value Added, Business Process Redesign, Product-Market Scan, and so on. These techniques are immensely powerful. They allow McKinsey consultants very rapidly to fit the raw data that lands on their desks into a coherent framework and give them insights into the nature of the client's problem. The consultants can then focus their thinking on the "drivers" of the problem and start working toward a solution.

We made frequent use of an analytical framework called Forces at Work. It proved especially valuable at the start of an engagement in helping us look at the likely external pressures on the client. The technique involves identifying the client's suppliers, customers, competitors, and possible substitute products. We then list all the changes occurring in each of the four categories. What impact— positive or negative—could these have on our client? Also, what internal changes are affecting the client and the client's industry? Which of these factors could actually cause major changes to the way the client designs, manufactures, distributes, sells, and services its products?

Whatever business you're in, this framework will not only help you build a snapshot of your competitive environment, but also help you develop a view of how that environment might change. Try it. It sounds simple, but it is a powerful way to stimulate your thinking about strategic business problems.

These frameworks really help at the start of the problem-solving process. For instance, when I was a second-year associate, I joined a team that was helping a major Wall Street investment bank reorganize its information technology department. All the executives at the bank wanted IT reorganized, but not if it meant any changes in the way *their* computers were supported. The IT department was a real mess, with 600 employees, a dozen different subdepartments, and a web of reporting relationships that made my head spin.

I (and the rest of the team) hardly knew where to begin. Fortunately, the Firm had recently developed a new paradigm, called Business Process Redesign, that gave us a starting point. The Firm was still coming to grips with BPR, and during the study we broke new ground for the Firm. It was hard work, but BPR (along with a lot of sweat, Chinese food, and late nights) helped us help the client force through the reorganization. If we had not had at least a starting framework to help us focus our efforts, we might never have left the ground.

... BUT EVERY CLIENT IS UNIQUE (NO COOKIE-CUTTER SOLUTIONS)

That there are many similarities between business problems does not mean that similar problems have similar solutions. You have to validate your initial hypothesis (or your gut) with fact-based analysis. This will put you in a much better position to get your ideas accepted.

If all you have is a hammer, then every problem looks like a nail. Critics of McKinsey (and management consulting in general) say that the Firm bases its solutions on the most current management fad—the favorite tool in its intellectual toolbox.

At the Firm, at least, this is untrue. Fact-based analysis as practiced by McKinsey requires hard proof before any recommendations are made to clients. Jason Klein, a former SEM at McKinsey and now publisher of *Field & Stream* and *Outdoor Life*, puts it like this:

> People think that the Firm—and management consultants in general—have a precanned answer. That is certainly not the

case at McKinsey; if it were, then the Firm would not be as successful as it is.

The tools may be the same from problem to problem, but you have to apply them. For instance, in my experience, in 8 out of 10 pricing problems the answer turns out to be "raise your prices." If you do the fact-based analysis—demand curves, breakeven calculations, budgets—enough times, you see almost invariably that firms should be raising their prices. But if you automatically say that's the answer, you'll get into trouble, because you'll run into an instance where the answer is really "lower your prices."

As a corollary to avoiding cookie-cutter solutions, be careful about blindly trusting your gut. As you gain experience in business, as you see and solve more and more problems, you will get a fair idea of what works in your industry and what doesn't. Although your gut will often be right, take a hint from former President Reagan: "Trust and verify." As a McKinsey alumnus who now works as a merchant banker put it:

A sharp manager with a lot of business experience can often reach the same conclusions as McKinsey—and in a much shorter time—by gut instinct, but most executives aren't that good. Because McKinsey focuses so intently on a problem, it often produces a more robust solution than even the best executive can. Most executives will miss a few things because they don't take the time—they usually don't have the time.

So, even though your initial instinct may be—and probably is —right, take enough time to verify your gut with facts.

DON'T MAKE THE FACTS FIT
YOUR SOLUTION

Avoid the temptation to view your initial hypothesis as the answer and the problem-solving process as an exercise in proving the IH. Keep an open and flexible mind. Don't let a strong initial hypothesis become an excuse for mental inflexibility.

On an engagement for a major insurance company, the EM assured his team and the client that the key to restoring the client's profitability was eliminating "leakage"—the acceptance of customer claims without adjustment. He assigned a new associate to determine the rate of leakage in fire insurance claims over the previous three years. As any good McKinsey associate would, this young man applied himself tirelessly and diligently to his task. He combed through stacks of claims in search of leakage. The result: very little leakage, far less than the EM had predicted.

Rather than take these data for what they were—an indication that he needed to reexamine his hypothesis—the EM simply told the young associate to look again, this time in auto insurance . . . and then in marine insurance . . . and in business insurance. Nowhere were the expected rates of leakage to be found.

One day, the EM was sitting in the team's on-site HQ looking slightly despondent. The team's main contact at the client poked his head around the doorpost. "What's the matter, Nick?" he said. "Not enough leakage for you?"

The moral of this little tale is that, no matter how brilliant, insightful, and original you may feel your initial hypothesis to be, you must always be prepared to accept that the facts may prove you wrong. If they do, adjust to the facts. Don't try to pound them into your framework like square pegs into round holes.

How do you avoid that trap? The McKinsey way is to take an occasional step back from the continual grind of fact gathering and analysis and to ask yourself what you have learned over the past week (or two weeks, or whatever). How does the new information fit into your initial hypothesis? If it doesn't, how might it change that hypothesis? Doing these little reality checks now and then could save you from chasing down blind alleys.

As a final note, I should add that the story, although true, represents the exception rather than the rule at McKinsey, at least in my experience. And that EM has long since left the Firm.

MAKE SURE YOUR SOLUTION FITS YOUR CLIENT

The most brilliant solution, backed up by libraries of data and promising billions in extra profits, is useless if your client or business can't implement it. Know your client. Know the organization's strengths, weaknesses, and capabilities—what management can and cannot do. Tailor your solutions with these factors in mind.

A former McKinsey EM who now works on Wall Street tells this story:

> We were doing a cost cutting study for a large financial institution. We discovered that they were in the midst of linking all their offices—they had several hundred around the world—by satellite. This project had begun several years

previously, and they had managed so far to roll it out to about half their offices.

We determined that with currently available technology they could do the same thing for a fraction of the cost using conventional phone lines. By our calculations, they would have saved $170 million on a present value basis.

We took our findings to the senior manager overseeing the engagement, the man who had brought us in to begin with, and he said, "Well, that's terrific. We appreciate that it could have saved us a few hundred million dollars, but we've already started down this road and, politically, it's just too risky. You have to realize that we only have a certain amount of energy in the organization and, frankly, we need ideas that are bigger than this."

At one level, it's unbelievable that he didn't accept our idea. But on another level, we were coming up with other suggestions that would save the organization half a billion or a billion dollars. So this was, if not exactly chicken feed, just a medium-size payoff for them. It's a rational response. If I can do only three things, I'll do the three biggest.

McKinsey hires people with stellar academic records and enforces a rigorous discipline in analyzing problems and structuring solutions. Because of this, a McKinsey-ite's (especially a new hire's) first instinct is to go hell for leather after the very best solution.

Unfortunately, when academic ideals meet business realities, business realities usually win. Businesses are full of real people, with real strengths and weaknesses and limitations. These people can do only so much with the finite resources available in their organizations. Some things they just cannot do, whether for political reasons, lack of resources or inability.

As a consultant, you bear the responsibility for knowing the limitations of your client; if your client is your own employer—or your own business—that responsibility is doubled. Knowing those limitations, you must make sure that any recommendations you make fit within them.

SOMETIMES YOU HAVE TO LET THE SOLUTION COME TO YOU

The McKinsey rules of problem solving, like all rules, have their exceptions. You will not be able to form an initial hypothesis every time. Sometimes, the client will not know what the problem is, just that there is a problem. Other times, the scope of your project will be so large—or so vague—that starting with an IH will be worthless. Still other times, you will be breaking new ground and nothing in your experience will point to a solution. Don't panic! If you get your facts together and do your analyses, the solution will come to you.

Hamish McDermott, former EM at the Firm, recounted this story:

> I was on a study where we were trying to improve the performance of the foreign exchange business of a major bank; we were supposed to reduce costs in the back-office operation by 30 percent. I had nothing at that stage that I could point to, no initial hypothesis about how to get those costs out of the organization. Frankly, we knew very little about how the back-office processing worked.

I had to interview the woman in charge of back-office processing along with her senior staff. She didn't mean to be unpleasant, although it certainly felt that way, but she came right out and said, "You've never done this before and you know nothing about this business. One of two things is going to happen. Either you'll come back with something we don't agree with, which will necessarily be wrong, or you'll listen to us and come back with what we already know, in which case you've added no value. We understand that you're here and that you're working on this, but from our point of view it's a total waste of our time and the bank's money."

Still, she gave us the data we asked for. It turned out that one product, which represented about 5 percent of their business, was producing about 50 percent of their costs. We were able to fix that. They'd had no idea this was going on. In subsequent stages of the engagement, we were able to extend this analysis to other parts of the business and we easily exceeded our targets.

The moral of this story is that an initial hypothesis is not a prerequisite for successful problem solving. Having one will help organize and forward your thinking, but if you can't come up with one, don't despair. Any McKinsey-ite will tell you that no business problem is immune to the power of fact-based analysis. Put together enough facts, combine them with some creative thinking, and you will come up with a solution.

SOME PROBLEMS YOU JUST CAN'T SOLVE . . . SOLVE THEM ANYWAY

Eventually, you will run into a brick wall that is tougher than your head. Don't keep pounding; it has no effect on the wall and does your head no good.

My unofficial mentor at McKinsey asked me to work with him on what promised to be a fun and exciting study. The client, a major financial institution in the midst of reorganizing its investment management business, faced severe challenges of heroic dimensions: thousands of employees, billions of dollars. The McKinsey team included my mentor and my favorite EM. It seemed the perfect recipe for an enjoyable, challenging McKinsey engagement.

The recipe might have been right, but the result left a bad taste in our mouths. Factions within the client's senior management prevented us from doing our job. Data we asked for arrived late, or in an unusable form or not at all. People we needed to interview refused to speak with us. The members of the client team vigorously pursued their own agendas at the expense of reaching a solution. We spent several uncomfortable months on this study and, in the end, had to make what recommendations we could, "declare victory," and get out.

My team's experience was hardly unique in the history of the Firm. The road of problem solving is often strewn with obstacles. Data to prove your hypothesis may be missing or bad. Sometimes businesses realize too late that they have a problem; by the time McKinsey, or anyone, addresses the problem, the business is already doomed.

The biggest obstacle—the troll guarding the bridge—is politics.

The first thing to understand about politics—and how it can help or hinder you from doing your job—is that businesses are full of real people. When you look at the boxes on an organization chart, you are really looking at people. When you move those boxes around, you change someone's life. As one former McKinsey EM remarked, "Sometimes change management means just that— changing management."

When members of a McKinsey team go into a client, they carry change with them. Some at the client will welcome the bringers of change as white knights riding to the rescue; others will see McKinsey as an invading army to either flee or drive out, depending on their power in the organization. As one former McKinsey-ite put it, "It was a rare engagement when there wasn't at least one sector of the client organization that did not want us there and did not want us to come up with a real answer."

In most cases, when senior management brings in McKinsey, enough players in the organization will cooperate willingly and McKinsey can be effective. A few malcontents may grumble or even cause trouble, but in the end they will be either converted to McKinsey's cause or bypassed. Sometimes, however, one powerful faction in an organization calls in McKinsey against the wishes of another powerful faction. That's when trouble arises, as we found out.

You have several options to pick from when confronted by a problem that seems too difficult to solve.

Redefine the problem. You can tell your client that the problem is not X, it's Y. This is especially useful when you know that solving Y will add a lot of value, where as trying to wrestle with X would cost a lot of time and resources for little result. If you make this switch very early on, you show great business judgment; if you do it after several weeks" work, you risk being accused of a cop out.

Tweak your way to a solution. Sometimes you will come up with a great solution that you know the client organization cannot implement. This is especially true with organizational change—it is easy to devise an optimal organization, but you usually have to deal with the personnel resources that the client already has. When that happens to you, expand your time horizon. Don't worry about implementing your solution immediately. As people leave the organization, you can "tweak" your way to your optimum over time.

Work through the politics. Even political problems are soluble. Most people in business are rational, at least in their business conduct. They react to incentives. Therefore, when you face political opposition, it usually means that your solution has negative implications for someone in the organization. So politics is just people acting in their own interests.

To work through the politics, you must think about how your solution affects the players in an organization. You must then build a consensus for change that takes account of the different incentives and organizational factors driving the politics. Consensus building may require you to change your solution to make it acceptable. Do it. Remember that politics is the art of the possible, and it's no good devising the ideal solution if the client refuses to accept it.

3

80/20 AND OTHER RULES TO LIVE BY

This chapter contains a number of rules that McKinsey consultants have found useful when trying to solve problems. They are difficult to classify. Call them my "Other Issues."

80/20

The 80/20 rule is one of the great truths of management con-
sulting and, by extension, of business. You will see it wher-
ever you look: 80 percent of your sales will come from 20
percent of your sales force; 20 percent of a secretary's job will
take up 80 percent of her time; 20 percent of the population
controls 80 percent of the wealth. It doesn't always work
(sometimes the bread falls butter-side up), but if you keep
your eyes peeled for examples of 80/20 in your business, you
will come up with ways to improve it.

I saw the 80/20 rule at work all the time at McKinsey, and I've
always been impressed by its power as a problem-solving rule
of thumb.

In my first-ever McKinsey study, when I was between years at
business school, I joined a team working with a large New York
brokerage house. The board of directors wanted McKinsey to
show them how to improve the profitability of their institutional
equity brokerage business—the selling of stocks to large pension
funds and mutual funds like Fidelity and T. Rowe Price.

When a client asks the question "How do I boost my profits?"
the first thing McKinsey does is take a step back and ask the question "Where do your profits come from?" The answer to this is not
always obvious, even to people who have been in their particular
business for years. To answer this question for our client, our team
went through *every* account of *every* broker and *every* trader by
customer. We spent several weeks analyzing this mountain of data
from every conceivable angle, but when we ran the numbers there
are some of the first things we saw:

- 80 percent of the sales came from 20 percent of the brokers.
- 80 percent of the orders came from 20 percent of the customers.
- 80 percent of the trading profit came from 20 percent of the traders.

These results pointed to some serious problems in the way the client allocated its staff resources, and we focused on those like a laser. Once we started digging, we found that the situation was more complex than simply "80 percent of the sales staff is lazy or incompetent" (not that we ever thought that was the case to begin with). We discovered, to give one example, that our client's three top brokers handled the 10 biggest accounts. By sharing these big accounts out among more brokers, and by dedicating one senior and one junior broker to each of the three largest customers, we actually increased total sales from these accounts. Rather than divide up the pie more fairly, we increased the size of the pie. Thus, 80/20 gave us a jump-start in solving the client's problem.

80/20 is all about data. What are your sales figures by product? What is your margin by product? How does each member of your sales team perform in terms of sales? In terms of profits? What is the success rate of your research teams? What is the geographical distribution of your customers? If you know your business well (and you'd better if you want to survive), then you know the right questions to ask. When you have your data, put it on a spreadsheet or in a database. Sort it in various ways. Play with the numbers. You will begin to see patterns, clumps that stand out. Those patterns will highlight aspects of your business that you probably did not realize. They may mean problems (a big problem if 80 percent of your profits come from 20 percent of your product lines), but they also mean opportunities. Find the opportunities and make the most of them.

DON'T BOIL THE OCEAN

Work smarter, not harder. There's a lot of data out there relating to your problem, and a lot of analyses you could do. Ignore most of them.

McKinsey gathers enough facts to prove or disprove a hypothesis or support or refute an analysis—and only enough facts. This is the flip side of fact-based analysis in a business situation. Anything more is a waste of time and effort when both are precious commodities.

I had this lesson brought home to me late one night while I was drafting a "fact pack" on a client's competitor. I had gathered a mountain of data and was trying to wring out a few new insights from it. My EM, Vik, walked into my office, briefcase and coat in hand, and asked how my work was going. I told him it was going well, but I thought I could pull together a few more charts. He picked up my draft, leafed through it, and said, "Ethan, it's eleven o'clock. The client will love this. No one will be able to absorb more than you have here. Call it a day. Don't boil the ocean." We shared a cab home.

"Don't boil the ocean" means don't try to analyze everything. Be selective; figure out the priorities of what you are doing. Know when you have done enough, then stop. Otherwise, you will spend a lot of time and effort for very little return, like boiling the ocean to get a handful of salt.

FIND THE KEY DRIVERS

Many factors affect your business. Focus on the most important ones—the key drivers.

In any McKinsey team meeting where problem solving is on the agenda, someone will use the inelegant phrase "key drivers," as in, "Vik, I think these are the key drivers of this issue." In other words, there may be a 100 different factors affecting the sales of our widgets—weather, consumer confidence, raw material prices—but the three most important ones are X, Y, and Z. We'll ignore the rest.

Engineers learn something called the Square Law of Computation. It states that for every component of a system—for every additional equation in a problem—the amount of computation required to solve the system increases at least as fast as the square of the number of equations. In other words, if the complexity of your problem doubles, the time it takes to solve it quadruples—*unless you make some simplifications.* For example, our solar system contains millions of objects, all having gravitational effects on one another. When analyzing planetary motion, astronomers start by ignoring most of these objects.*

Focusing on the key drivers means drilling down to the core of the problem, rather than picking the whole problem apart piece by piece, layer by layer. Then, you can apply thorough, fact-based analysis where it will do the most good and avoid going down blind alleys.

---

*For an in-depth discussion of the square law of computation and other issues of complexity and problem solving, see Gerald M. Weinberg, *An Introduction to General Systems Thinking* (New York: John Wiley & Sons, 1975).

Syntactical foibles aside, "key drivers" is a very powerful concept. It saves you time. It saves you effort. It keeps you from boiling the ocean.

THE ELEVATOR TEST

Know your solution (or your product or business) so thoroughly that you can explain it clearly and precisely to your client (or customer or investor) in 30 seconds. If you can do that, then you understand what you're doing well enough to sell your solution.

Imagine it's time for that big, end-of-engagement presentation. You and your team have been up until 2 a.m. putting together your blue books,* making sure that every *i* has been dotted and every *t* crossed. You're all wearing your best suits and trying to look on the ball. The senior executives of your Fortune 50 client, anxious to hear McKinsey's words of wisdom, are taking their places around the boardroom table on the top floor of the corporate skyscraper. The CEO strides into the room and says, "Sorry, folks. I can't stay. We have a crisis and I have to go meet with our lawyers." Then he turns to you and says, "Why don't you ride down in the elevator with me and tell me what you've found out?" The ride will take about 30 seconds. In that time, can you tell the CEO your solution? Can you *sell* him your solution? That's the elevator test.

Many companies use the elevator test (or something similar) because it's an excellent way of making sure that their executives'

---

*A McKinsey presentation document so called because it is bound with blue cardboard covers.

time gets used efficiently. Procter & Gamble tells its managers to write one-page memos. A Hollywood producer will tell a screenwriter to "give me the bullet" on a new script; if, after 30 seconds, the producer likes what she's heard, the writer will get a chance to talk further, and maybe make a sale. Jason Klein instituted the elevator test when he took over as president of *Field & Stream*:

> My sales force could not explain the magazine to customers. Our advertisement space was shrinking. Then I trained my entire sales force on the elevator test. I challenged them to explain the magazine to me in 30 seconds. It became a valuable tool for them, and our ad base has grown every year.

How do you encapsulate six months' work in 30 seconds? Start with the issues that your team addressed. The client wants to know the recommendations for each issue and the payoff. If you have a lot of recommendations, stick to the three most important—the ones with the biggest payoffs. Don't worry about the supporting data; you can talk about that when you have more time.

For example, your analysis shows that a manufacturing client can't sell enough widgets because its sales force is organized by territory when it should be organized by buyer category. You have lots of data illustrating this: analyses of salespeople by buyer type, buyer interviews, field visits to retail and wholesale outlets, and so forth. When you're on that elevator ride, just tell the CEO, "We think you can boost sales of widgets by 50 percent in three years if you reorganize your sales force by buyer category. We can talk about the details later. Good luck with the lawyers."

PLUCK THE LOW-HANGING FRUIT

Sometimes in the middle of the problem-solving process, opportunities arise to get an easy win, to make immediate improvements, even before the overall problem has been solved. Seize those opportunities! They create little victories for you and your team. They boost morale and give you added credibility by showing anybody who may be watching that you're on the ball and mean business.

Whenever possible, McKinsey consultants put this doctrine into practice. Clients can get very impatient for a result during the six months (or more) that a big McKinsey engagement can last. Giving the client something practical before the end helps reduce the pressure on the team.

At my stockbroker client, after we had derived a number of insights (thanks to 80/20) from our analysis of sales and trading data, we wanted to communicate our findings to the senior managers of the institutional equities department. We set up a meeting with the department head and the heads of all the business units in the division: sales, trading, research, and so on.

Since I had taken the lead in the actual analysis of the data, I got to present our findings. They hit this group of very experienced Wall Street executives like a hammer. The client had no idea just how inefficient its operation was.

The presentation had two important effects. First, it convinced those executives who had not been particularly keen on McKinsey's presence in the first place that they had a problem and we could help solve it. Second, because I had presented the findings, their opinion of me rose quite sharply and my job became a lot easier. Before the meeting, I was some smart-ass MBA poking around their business. After the meeting, I was someone who was working for them to solve their problems.

By plucking the low-hanging fruit, by resisting the temptation to hoard our information until some big end-of-study presentation, we made our client more enthusiastic, our jobs easier, and ourselves happier.

This rule is really about satisfying your customer in a long-term relationship. Your customer could be the purchaser of your products, or it could be a client for your services, or it could be your boss. Whoever it is, it pays to keep him happy and let him know that he is your top priority. If you are on, say, a software design project with a three-month lead time and you've put together a usable program that solves part of the problem in two weeks, show it to your boss. Don't wait! Solving only part of a problem can still mean increased profits. Just don't let anybody think you've given up on a complete solution. Those little wins help you and your customers.

MAKE A CHART EVERY DAY

During the problem-solving process, you learn something new every day. Put it down on paper. It will help you push your thinking. You may use it, or you may not, but once you have crystalized it on the page, you won't forget it.

Making a chart every day may strike you as somewhat anal-retentive. It is. Then again, when you are trying to craft facts into solutions, that is not so bad.

In the course of a typical day at McKinsey, you could start with a quick brainstorming session at 9 a.m., move on to a client interview at 10, a factory tour at 11, and then a sandwich lunch with your director. You might follow this with more client interviews, an end-of-day team meeting, and then a quick trip down to Wharton to participate in a recruiting seminar. In the midst of all this, it is very easy for the facts to blend into one another like pools of different-colored inks on a sheet of blotting paper. Even if you take good notes at your interviews and have the minutes of your team meetings, important points could get lost.

You can avoid this by sitting down for half an hour at the end of the day and asking yourself, "What are the three most important things I learned today?" Put them down in a chart or two—nothing fancy; neatness doesn't count. If the facts don't lend themselves to charting (although McKinsey-ites try to put everything in charts), just write them down as bullet points. Put your results someplace where they won't get lost—don't just toss them into your in-tray. Later, when you are in analysis mode, you can come back to your charts and notes and think about what they mean and where they fit in terms of your solution.

Of course, this little tip can be taken too far. One EM from Germany, while working out of the New York office, would write a whole *presentation* every night. I wouldn't recommend this for most people—at least those with a life. Then again, the EM was far from home, didn't know anyone in town, and had nothing better to do. He should have followed some of the suggestions presented in Part Four.

HIT SINGLES

You can't do everything, so don't try. Just do what you're supposed to do and get it right. It's much better to get to first base consistently than to try to hit a home run—and strike out 9 times out of 10.

Shortly after I joined McKinsey, the New York office held a retreat at a resort upstate. One day we associates had to interrupt our strenuous regimen of golf, paintball, and wine tasting to hear a lecture (hey, you have to do some work at these things). The speaker was the CEO of a major electronics company, a client of the Firm, and a McKinsey alumnus himself. His main message was "Don't try to knock the ball out of the park. Hit singles. Get your job done—don't try to do the work of the whole team."

His speech took me by surprise. McKinsey associates have spent their whole lives "knocking it out of the park." They all have first-class academic backgrounds combined with records of achievement in other fields. They had to impress a group of sharp-eyed and skeptical McKinsey consultants just to make it past the first job interview at the Firm. To gear down upon joining would strike most of them as strange, if not distasteful.

It took several years of gaining perspective before I understood the wisdom of the CEO's words. There are three reasons he was right:

- It's impossible to do everything yourself all the time.
- If you manage it once, you raise unrealistic expectations from those around you.
- Once you fail to meet expectations, it is very difficult to regain credibility.

It's impossible to do everything yourself all the time. Business problems are complicated—the problems McKinsey deals with especially so. If you don't leverage the other members of your team to solve these problems, you are wasting valuable resources. The principle applies as much to senior managers as to junior executives whose MBA diplomas are still wet with ink. Very few people have the brainpower and energy to be a one-man show all the time.

If you manage it once, you raise unrealistic expectations from those around you. Suppose, for a moment, that you manage, through superhuman effort, to perform well beyond what is normally expected of you. You hit that ball out of the park and (what the heck) the bases were loaded. Congratulations. Of course, now your boss or your shareholders will expect you to do the same thing every time you step up to the plate.

Once you fail to meet expectations, it is very difficult to regain credibility. At McKinsey, it is said that you are only as good as your last study. If you have one "bad" engagement, all your hard work before that doesn't matter. EMs won't want you on their teams. You won't be staffed on the interesting projects. You won't be put in a position to excel. Your career at the Firm will suffer. Prepare your résumé.

The same thing happens in the stock market. A high-flying company that posts 20 percent profit increases every year sees its stock price soar. When it misses one quarter, even by as little as a cent, its momentum reverses. Wall Street drops the stock like a hot potato and its share price plummets. After that, even when the company gets back on the growth track, several years can go by before investors trust it enough to pile back in.

When I was a kid, I had a fantasy baseball board game. You picked your team from a combination of then current players (Carl Yastrzemski, Sandy Koufax, Roberto Clemente) and baseball legends (Ruth, Cobb, DiMaggio). Each player came on a circle of paper marked out in sections printed with a result: single, double, home run, strikeout, and so forth. The size of each section depended on the player's career record. To play the game, you'd put the circle around a little pointer and spin the pointer; wherever it landed was the result for that player's turn at bat. The one thing I remember from that game was that the home run kings like Ruth, DiMaggio, and Aaron had the biggest strikeout zones too.

It's all very well to talk of the necessity to strive purposefully and, if you fail, to fail gloriously. It's OK for Mark McGwire to strike out a lot, as long as he keeps hitting those home runs. In the business world, though, you're much better off hitting singles.

LOOK AT THE BIG PICTURE

Every now and then, take a mental step back from whatever you're doing. Ask yourself some basic questions: How does what you're doing solve the problem? How does it advance your thinking? Is it the most important thing you could be doing right now? If it's not helping, why are you doing it?

When you are trying to solve a difficult problem for your client or company, you can easily lose sight of your goal amid the million and one demands on your time. It's like you are hip-deep in a bog, following a muddy channel that you can't see. Analysis B follows analysis A and seems in turn to be followed seamlessly by analysis C. New data comes in and points to yet more analyses with which to fill your days (and nights).

When you're feeling swamped by it all, take a metaphorical step back and figure out what it is you're trying to achieve. Do this by looking at "the big picture": the set of issues that make up your operating hypothesis. How does what you're doing fit into the big picture? A particular analysis may be intellectually correct, even interesting, but if it doesn't take you closer to a solution, it's a waste of time. Figure out your priorities; you can do only so much in a day. There is nothing quite so frustrating as looking back over the course of a day or week and realizing, not that you haven't come up with any end products, but that what you have come up with is worthless in terms of the problem at hand.

As one former McKinsey EM told me, "Perhaps the most valuable thing I learned during my time at the Firm was to think about the big picture—to take a step back, figure out what I'm trying to achieve, and then look at whatever I'm doing and ask myself, 'Does this really matter?'"

JUST SAY, "I DON'T KNOW"

The Firm pounds the concept of professional integrity into its associates from their first day on the job, and rightly so. One important aspect of professional integrity is honesty—with your clients, your team members, and yourself. Honesty includes recognizing when you haven't got a clue. Admitting that is a lot less costly than bluffing.

It was the morning of an important progress meeting at our client, a Fortune 50 manufacturing company. The team and John, our ED,* were going over the various sections of the presentation. I

---

*Engagement director, also called a partner. The ED is in charge of a study, and most EDs head up several studies at one time. EDs have an equity stake in the Firm.

had already been through my piece of it; I had been up until 4 a.m. getting it ready and I was exhausted. As the discussion moved to another section, one that I had nothing to do with and knew little about, my brain started slipping into that blissful place known as sleep. I could hear the other members of the team discussing various points, but their words slipped away from my mind like water through a child's cupped fingers.

Suddenly, my reverie evaporated as John asked me, "So, Ethan, what do you think about Suzie's point?" Momentary shock and fear yielded to concentration as I tried to recall what had just been said. Years of Ivy League and business school reflexes took over and I came out with a few lines of general agreement. Of course, what I said might just as well have come out of a horse's backside.

If I had told John, "I'm not really sure—I haven't looked at this issue before," I would have been fine. Even if I had said, "Sorry, I just lost it for a minute," he would have understood; after all, he had been through exactly the same experience, like every other McKinsey-ite. Instead, I tried to fake it, and ended up slipping in my own horsefeathers.

At the end of the engagement, several weeks later, the team had its final party. We went out to TGI Friday's, ate a lot of nachos, and drank a lot of beer. Then the EM began presenting each of the team members with presents of a rude and/or humorous nature. For my gift, he handed me a little desktop picture frame around the following words, neatly printed in the McKinsey official font: "Just say, 'I don't know.'"

This is sage advice, and that picture frame remains on my desk to this day.

DON'T ACCEPT "I HAVE NO IDEA"

People always have an idea if you probe just a bit. Ask a few pointed questions—you'll be amazed at what they know. Combine that with some educated guessing, and you can be well along the road to the solution.

If you ask people a question about their business and they tell you, "I have no idea," don't just walk away in defeat. "I have no idea" is a code; it really means, "I'm too busy to take the time to think about this," or "I don't think I'm smart enough to know about these things," or worst of all "I'm too lazy to come up with anything useful."

Don't accept "I have no idea"—treat it as a challenge. Like the sculptor who turned a block of marble into an elephant by chiseling away everything that didn't look like an elephant, you must chip away at "I have no idea" with pointed questions.

When Jason Klein wanted to put together a new business unit, he was sure that his top competitor was outspending him by a factor of 10. How could he prove this to his board of directors so they would give him more funding? He told his team to put together a P&L (profit and loss statement) for the competitor that showed what it was spending. As he recalls it:

> When I first suggested that we do this analysis, my people said, "We have no idea." So I challenged them. Did they know how much our competitor was spending on advertising? No, but they could make an educated guess. Did they know how much our competitor was spending on production costs? No, but they could make an estimate of the competitor's cost per issue and multiply that by reported circulation. And so it went.

In the end, we put together a pretty comprehensive P&L backed up by solid assumptions. It may have been off by a factor of 2, but who cares? What mattered was that it was accurate enough to make the business decision that was on the table.

Just as you shouldn't accept "I have no idea" from others, so you shouldn't accept it from yourself, or expect others to accept it from you. This is the flip side of "I don't know." With a bit of thinking and searching, you will usually find that you do know or can find out something about a question or issue (unless, of course, you have fallen asleep in the middle of a team meeting).

PART TWO

THE McKINSEY WAY OF WORKING TO SOLVE BUSINESS PROBLEMS

In Part One, we looked at the way McKinsey thinks about business problems and uses fact-based, hypothesis-driven, structured analysis to arrive at solutions for its clients. In Part Two, we will see how the Firm implements its problem-solving model on a day-to-day basis.

We will go through a McKinsey engagement in chronological order, starting with the selling (or, in McKinsey's case, nonselling) process, progressing to organizing a team, conducting research, and brainstorming.

The goal in Part Two is for you to experience what it's like to participate in a typical McKinsey study. I hope, however, that, unlike a typical McKinsey engagement, it won't take you six months of working until 1 a.m. to finish it.

4

SELLING A STUDY

ABOUT THE SELLING PROCESS AT McKINSEY

The selling process at McKinsey differs from that of most organizations because, as any McKinsey-ite will tell you, the Firm doesn't sell. The Firm may not sell, but it certainly brings in a continuing and growing volume of business, so there's something to be learned from the way McKinsey gets itself through its clients' doors.

Getting your foot through the door is only half the battle when marketing your skills as a problem solver, however. You also have to put together your problem-solving package in way that ensures your success. McKinsey has learned a thing or two about that as well. In this chapter, we will look at the Zen of McKinsey salesmanship and learn how to trim a problem-solving project to a manageable size and scope.

HOW TO SELL WITHOUT SELLING

Business problems are like mice. They go unnoticed until they start nibbling your cheese. Just building a better mousetrap will not make the world beat a path to your door. People who don't have mice won't be interested—until the mice show up; then they need to know you have the mousetrap. This might sound like the musings of a Zen monk (or perhaps a management consultant from California). But sometimes the right way to sell your product or service is not to barge into your customer's home with a bunch of free samples. Just be there, at the right time, and make sure the right people know who you are.

At around 10 one evening, I went up to the office of Dominic, the partner on my team, to drop off some documents that I knew he wanted to see in the morning. To my surprise, he was still at his desk. When I asked what kept him so late, he told me he had a "beauty parade" for a prospective client the next morning.

"Good luck," I told him as I left. "I hope you sell them on this one."

"No, no," he replied. "Remember, McKinsey doesn't sell."

This dictum may sound strange. How could a company grow to the size of McKinsey without selling? But it is true. This curious aspect of McKinsey's culture stems from the roots of the Firm's founders in "white shoe" law and accounting firms before World War II. In those days, it was considered beneath the dignity of professional service firms to advertise or solicit business.

Times may have changed, but the no-selling legacy persists at McKinsey because it works very well in the consulting business.

No senior McKinsey directors make cold calls at the offices of Bill Gates and Ted Turner asking if they have problems they want solved. The Firm does not run ads in *Forbes* or *Barron's* advertising 50 percent off telecommunications consulting. Although a partner's compensation depends in large part on the amount of business he brings to the Firm, no one goes out to knock on doors. The Firm waits for the phone to ring.

And ring it does, not because McKinsey sells, but because McKinsey *markets*. It does this in several different ways, all of them designed to make sure that on the day a senior executive decides she has a business problem, one of the first calls she makes is to the local office of McKinsey. The Firm produces a steady stream of books and articles, some of them extremely influential, such as the famous *In Search of Excellence* by Peters and Waterman.* McKinsey also publishes its own scholarly journal, *The McKinsey Quarterly*, which it sends gratis to its clients, as well as to its former consultants, many of whom now occupy senior positions at potential clients. The Firm invites (and gets) a lot of coverage by journalists. Many McKinsey partners and directors are internationally known as experts in their fields. Examples are Lowell Bryan, who has advised congressional banking committees, and Kenichi Ohmae (who recently left the Firm), the business guru whose nickname in Japanese is "Keiei no Kamisama"—the God of Management.

McKinsey maintains a vast network of informal contacts with potential clients as well. The Firm encourages its partners to participate in "extracurricular activities" such as sitting on the boards of charities, museums, and cultural organizations; many members of these boards are executives at current or potential clients. McKinsey consultants also address industry conferences.

---

*Thomas J. Peters and Robert H. Waterman, Jr., *In Search of Excellence: Lessons from America's Best-Run Companies* (New York: Harper&Row, 1982).

Occasional meetings with former clients allow partners not only to check up on the effects of past McKinsey projects, but to make sure that the Firm maintains some "share of mind" should new problems arise at the client.

These efforts could not be construed as selling, but they make sure that the right people know the Firm is there. That keeps the phones ringing.

If you're in sales, then you probably do have to make the cold calls. For some people that is the fun of selling. But even the best foot-in-the-door saleswoman needs to market.

You may not be on the same charitable board as billionaire investor Warren Buffett, but you can still find ways to network with existing and potential clients and customers. Trade shows, and conferences, even the right bars, will give you the chance to make sure they know who you are. Does your particular field have a trade journal? These magazines are always looking for copy from industry insiders: Write a good article and you will get your name in front of people who would otherwise never have heard of you. Meet your competitors too. Today's competitor could change jobs and become tomorrow's customer. Make sure he knows you! It all adds up to making sure your name is the one your customers think of when they have a need you can fill.

BE CAREFUL WHAT YOU PROMISE: STRUCTURING AN ENGAGEMENT

When structuring your project, whether you are selling your services as a consultant or have been picked by your organization to solve an internal problem, don't bite off more than you can chew. Set definite milestones that you can meet. That way, you'll have targets you can achieve and your client will be satisfied.

When clients come to McKinsey with a problem, they want it fixed yesterday and for nothing. Fortunately, most clients realize that this desire is just slightly unrealistic. Still, when structuring an engagement, McKinsey (usually in the person of a DCS* or ED) faces a lot of pressure to deliver the maximum results in the minimum time. McKinsey bills by the hour, and those hours do not come cheap.

The ED (or whoever is structuring the engagement) stands between the client and its demands on one side, and the engagement team on the other. The team can be pushed only so far for so long before the quality of its work begins to decline. McKinsey consultants, in general, work very hard over the course of a study, but they do have limits; they also have lives, which they would like, at least occasionally, to live. The challenge for the ED is to balance the desires and budget constraints of the client with the limits of the team. The ideal synthesis of these two opposing forces is a project that a team of four to six consultants can com-

---

*Director of client services, a.k.a. director. The DCS is in charge of the overall relationship with a client. Directors have a larger stake in the Firm than mere partners. The DCS is the highest rung of the McKinsey hierarchy.

plete in three to six months and that will produce *tangible results* for the client.

As the Firm spends time within a client organization, it almost always uncovers new problems that could benefit from McKinsey's expertise. These problems, however must be addressed at another time and in another engagement. Consequently, McKinsey engagements tend to generate new business of their own accord. Thus, as long as the client is happy with the results that the Firm produces, McKinsey is likely to have a stream of new business (for which it often will not need to compete).

As an organization, McKinsey is extremely good at figuring out how much a team can do over the length of a typical study. The best EDs can balance the competing demands of client and team to a nicety; they tell the client, "We're going to do X and Y. We could do Z, but it would kill the team," while telling the team, "Look, we've already promised the client that we would do Z, so we've got to deliver." They then work the team to its limit while simultaneously making the client feel that he is getting value for money and exceeding his expectations.

Of course, not every ED is that good. In my time at the Firm, certain EDs had reputations for overpromising to the client and then putting their teams through hell. They were to be avoided, along with EDs who were vague about the exact nature of the end product of a study and left the team to figure out just what it was supposed to do.

What lessons does the McKinsey experience give for the way you should structure your problem-solving project? If you are a consultant putting together a proposal for an outside client, then the answer is simple: Don't bite off more than you (and your team) can chew and know what your end product is going to be.

If your boss steps into your office and says, "We have a little problem and we want you to head up a team to solve it," then the lesson for you is a bit more complicated. Don't blithely accept the assignment and say, "Sure, boss." If you do, you could be setting yourself up for a fall.

Before you go hot footing it in search of a solution, get a feel for the scope of the problem. Is it something you and your team can solve in the time allotted? If not, either get more time or, even better, sit down with your boss and break the problem down into bite-size chunks. Figure out what the end product of each chunk will be: a recommendation, an implementation plan, a new product design, and so forth. Figure out what resources you will need to reach your goal and get a commitment from your boss that you will have them. Doing all this ahead of time can save you a lot of grief a few months down the road.

Structuring your project properly at the beginning may not guarantee your success, but it at least gets you off to the right start.

5

ASSEMBLING A TEAM

ABOUT TEAMS AT McKINSEY

At McKinsey, you never walk alone—or, at least, you never work alone. Everything at the Firm happens in teams, from front-line work on client engagements all the way up to firmwide decision making. The smallest team I ever worked on consisted of me and my EM on a pro bono engagement for a New York theater company. At the other end of the scale, the Firm's largest clients might have several five- or six-person teams working on site at one time; together, these form a "metateam." In the early 1990s, members of the AT&T metateam decided to get together to discuss their work; the Firm's headquarters didn't have a room large enough to hold them all, so they had to book a New Jersey hotel.

McKinsey relies on teams because they are the best way to solve the problems that the Firm's clients face. The complexity of these problems makes it impossible for one person to solve them—at least to the Firm's high standards. More people mean more hands to gather and analyze data and, more important, more minds to figure out what the data really mean. If you face complex problems in your business, you should probably put together a team to help solve them too. In the face of complexity, many hands don't just make light work; they make for a better result.

The Firm has developed a number of strategies for putting together and maintaining high-performance teams. In this chapter, you will learn how to select the right people for your team. You will also discover some tricks for keeping your team happy and productive under pressure.

GETTING THE MIX RIGHT

You can't just throw four random people at a problem and expect them to solve it. Think about what sorts of skills and personalities will work best for your project. Then choose your teammates carefully.

To succeed as a business problem solver, you must choose your team carefully, getting the best mix of people from the resources you have available. McKinsey benefits from a global pool of talented, intelligent individuals whose strengths and weaknesses the Firm tracks closely. Even with this advantage, EMs and EDs must learn the art of team selection. Their experiences can help you, even if you can't call on the same level of resources.

McKinsey-ites subscribe to one of two theories of team selection. The first theory states that intellectual horsepower is everything—find the smartest people for your team regardless of their experience or personal hygiene. The second theory says that what really matters is specific experience and skills; intelligence is a given within the Firm—every McKinsey consultant is smart or he wouldn't be there.

Neither of these theories is completely correct, but neither of them is completely wrong either. Proper team selection varies from problem to problem and client to client. Some problems will yield only to large amounts of analytical firepower. For instance, if you have mountains of complex data that you need to decipher, then you want the two or three best number crunchers that you can find, regardless of whether they can simultaneously walk and chew gum. On the other hand, if you are managing a big reorganization during which many sensitive decisions will have to be made, you would prefer to have someone on your team with good people skills and experience in implementing change.

Another important team selection lesson emerges from the McKinsey team assignment process. When an engagement begins, the EM and ED pick their associates from the pool of available resources at the time. The "manager of associate development" or the office manager will tell them who is available and give them a sheet listing each associate's experience and rating each one on analytical ability, client management skills, and so forth. The biggest mistake in team selection comes from taking those ratings at face value. A smart EM *always* talks to potential team members before taking them on.

By extension, if you are in a position to pick your team members before embarking on a project, never just accept people who are *supposed* to be good. Meet them face to face. Talk to them; see what's behind the recommendations. Maybe in her last assignment Sally just got lucky. Or maybe Pete's the CEO's nephew and his last boss was scared to tell the truth about him. (Of course, if he is the CEO's nephew, you may be stuck with him.) Maybe Carol's brilliant, but after spending 15 minutes talking to her, you know she would drive you crazy if she were on your team.

Just remember, if you are lucky enough to be able to choose whom you will work with, choose wisely.

A LITTLE TEAM BONDING GOES A LONG WAY

It's a truism that a team will perform better and its members will have a better time if the team members get along well. As a team leader, you should make an effort to promote team bonding; just make sure it doesn't become a chore.

For McKinsey-ites, team-bonding activities are a given. In the course of an engagement, you expect to go out at least a few times to the nicest restaurants in town, or to see a show or a game on McKinsey's (and, eventually, the client's) nickel. One ED even took his whole team to Florida for a long weekend.

As a team leader, the question for you is how much formal team bonding is enough. After talking with a number of former McKinsey-ites, and reflecting on my own experience, I'm going to go out on a limb and say that the answer is not much. A little team bonding goes a long way. As a team leader, you have the far more important job of looking after team morale (see the next section). Former SEM Abe Bleiberg put it like this:

> I'm not sure that team bonding is all that important. What's important is that a team works together well, and that will come or not over the course of a project. It's also important that individuals feel respected and that they feel that their ideas are respected.
>
> Team bonding is not, "Did you take your team to enough dinners? Did you go out to the movies? Did you go to the circus?" Most people, even very hard-working people, want to have a life, to be with their families. I think that's more important than going out to the circus.

If a team is going to bond, it will mostly bond through work. A typical McKinsey team works at the client for 10 to 14 hours a day, plus a day over the weekend at the office. That's plenty of time for bonding. Also, on an out-of-town study, team members will eat dinner together more often than not. Why, as a team leader, would you want to take up yet more of their time? If the team isn't bonding, how is a fancy dinner going to help? Will it make a bad work experience good?

So, when managing your team, be selective with team-bonding activities. Try to get your team's "significant others" involved; this will help them understand what their loved ones—your teammates—are doing, and it will help *you* understand your teammates. Above all, respect your teammates' time. One former associate noted that, at McKinsey, the best team dinners were at lunch —they showed that the EM knew the associates had lives.

TAKE YOUR TEAM'S TEMPERATURE TO MAINTAIN MORALE

Maintaining your team's morale is an on-going responsibility. If you don't do it, your team will not perform well. Make sure you know how your team feels.

In my time at McKinsey, I worked on two studies that didn't turn out well. Both studies were charged with client politics—the McKinsey team became a football kicked between rival factions at the client. After one of the studies, I recognized that we hadn't succeeded and I was ready to move on to the next engagement.

After the other, I was ready to leave the Firm.* Why the different reactions? Team morale.

My "bad" EM (who shall remain nameless) managed by the Mushroom Method: "Cover them with manure and keep them in the dark." We associates never felt that we knew what was going on; I never got a sense that what I was doing was valuable, either to the team or to the client. My "good" EM, on the other hand, always let us know what was going on, and if he didn't know, Vik told us so. We knew about the client politics—we understood it—and that made it easier for us to work with it. Also, I knew that Vik's door was always open and that he was pulling for us as much as for the client.**

What's the secret to maintaining team morale? There isn't one—just a few simple rules to remember.

Take your team's temperature. Talk to your teammates. Make sure they are happy with what they are doing. Find out if they have questions about what they are doing or why they are doing it, and answer them. If they are unhappy, take remedial action quickly.

Steer a steady course. If you change your mind all the time about the team's priorities or the analyses you're doing, your team will quickly become confused and demoralized. Know where you're going and stay your course. If you need an extra day to figure it out, take it. If you need to make a big change, let your team know, explain why, and let people contribute to, or at least see, your thought process.

Let your teammates know why they are doing what they're doing. People want to feel that what they are doing is adding value to the client. There are few things more demoralizing than doing something that you *and* your team leader know is valueless. No

---

*I didn't. I went skiing in Vail for a week instead. I felt better after that.
**Both EMs eventually made partner—a comment, perhaps, on which skills the Firm values most in its EDs.

one on your team should ever feel, "I've just spent two weeks of my life for nothing."

Treat your teammates with respect. There is no excuse for treating people with disrespect; it's completely unprofessional. Respect doesn't just mean politeness. It means remembering that your teammates may have different priorities than you do, and that they may have lives outside of work. You may like to work until midnight six days a week, but your team may have better things to do. There will be times, of course, when the team must work all hours, but be sure it really is one of those times before you call a team meeting at 10 p.m. Respect also means never asking someone to do something you wouldn't do or haven't done yourself. As an associate, I always felt a bit better knowing that if I was in the office at midnight, my EM was too.

Get to know your teammates as people. Are they married? Do they have kids? What are their hobbies? It will help you to understand them. Share a bit about yourself as well; that makes it more likely that your teammates will think of you as part of "us," rather than "them." This, incidentally, is a much better way of team bonding than taking your team out to the ball game.

When the going gets tough, take the Bill Clinton approach. Sometimes, as in my two bad experiences, you will be dealt a bad hand. The problem is difficult; the client is difficult. There's not a lot you can do beyond telling your team, "I feel your pain." At some point, you have to soldier on; that's life.

Spending months solving complex business problems is no bed of roses. If you follow the rules on maintaining morale, however, at least your team won't feel like resigning when it's all over.

6

MANAGING HIERARCHY

ABOUT THE McKINSEY CHAIN OF COMMAND

McKinsey has something of a split personality when it comes to hierarchy. On the one hand, the Firm claims that it has no real hierarchy. On the other hand, any McKinsey-ite past or present can tell you that two hierarchies (at least) exist within McKinsey. Both statements are correct.

I cannot imagine a flatter organization than McKinsey. I could, as an associate, walk into my ED's office without an appointment and talk to him about our study. In meetings at the Firm, every idea, whether it comes from the youngest business analyst or the oldest director, carries the same weight and is debated and attacked accordingly (at least that's the way it's supposed to be, and usually is).

At the same time, McKinsey has a definite chain of command. The directors and, to a lesser extent, the partners make decisions about the direction of the Firm, and the EMs, associates, analysts, and support staff live with them. If I disagreed with my EM over an issue, at the end of the day, his opinion won out. Likewise, my ED's opinion trumped my EM's.

Then, McKinsey has another, unofficial hierarchy: one based on experience and credentials—how good you are (or are perceived to be). At each level, certain people were known to be "stars." Stellar associates could pick and choose their assignments, while hot EMs had associates clamoring to work for them and everyone sought out the best EDs and DCSs as mentors and career makers. On the other hand, associates who performed poorly didn't last very long at the Firm—after one bad engagement, no EM or ED would want them on the team. Likewise, the associates generally knew which EMs to avoid and which EDs had missed the Firm's fast track.

Every organization has its own approach to hierarchy. Your own may look nothing at all like the Firm's. Still, every McKinsey-ite has learned a few lessons about dealing with hierarchy that should work in any organization. They can help you stay out of trouble and get ahead.

MAKE YOUR BOSS LOOK GOOD

If you make your boss look good, your boss will make you look good. That's the quid pro quo of hierarchy.

I was a first-year associate and I'd just spent several weeks putting together a comprehensive competitor analysis for my client. When it came time to share my findings with the senior management of a very hierarchical manufacturing company, I was too "green" to make the presentation. My EM got the job instead. I was disappointed, but I understood the rationale behind the decision.

It then became my job, over the course of several hours, to make my EM as conversant with my analysis as I was. The next day, he delivered the presentation very convincingly. When the client asked questions, my EM answered them; all the while, I was writing him notes, whispering facts in his ear, and pointing out important pages in the presentation document. The client was suitably impressed with the presentation and with my EM. My EM (my boss) and my ED (my boss's boss) were impressed with me. I had done my job and the Firm would know about it.

In any hierarchical organization, the most important person in your world, day in and day out, is your boss. When you work in teams, away from the main office, in a distant city or foreign country, that importance increases by an order of magnitude. Your boss may be the only person in your organization who can see you. You'd better make her happy. The best way to do that is to make her look good.

Making your boss look good means two things. Firstly, it means doing your job to the best of your ability. Clearly, if you produce high-quality work, it will make your boss's job easier.

Second, make sure your boss knows everything you know when she needs to know it. Keep the information flowing. Make sure your boss knows where you are, what you are doing, and what problems you may be having. At the same time, don't overload her with information. Think about what your boss needs or wants to know. Use a well-structured e-mail or voice mail to convey the information.

Getting these things right helps you as much as it helps your boss. To paraphrase a famous hairdresser, if your boss looks good, you look good.

AN AGGRESSIVE STRATEGY FOR MANAGING HIERARCHY

If you have the stomach for it, assert your equality in the organization. Keep on doing it until someone tells you otherwise. Obviously, this is not a strategy for everyone.

Hamish McDermott, a newly hired associate fresh from a graduate degree in philosophy at Cambridge, found himself assigned to an internal research project—what McKinsey calls practice development, or PD—for Lowell Bryan, a director of the Firm and a very imposing presence. Lowell had just finished the second chapter of a book on bank failures and asked Hamish and the rest of the team for their comments. Hamish took Lowell at his word and proceeded to write an account of all the logical flaws in the chapter. As Hamish remembers it:

> There I was, after a week at the Firm, showing the head of
> the finance practice exactly where he was being logically

inconsistent and where his arguments were failing. Of course, I had used a very dry, superior tone, as if it were an exam question at Cambridge: "So-and-so has made a valiant effort to expound his thesis, but failed for the following 16 reasons."

Lowell was working out of town at the time, and Hamish faxed his comments directly to him, without showing them to his EM. In many firms, this would have been enough to get Hamish the sack, but Lowell was fine with it. Hamish's EM later commented that maybe he should have been more careful about the tone of his comments. In fact, when the book came out, Lowell gave Hamish a copy inscribed with the message "Thanks for all your help, especially with Chapter 2." Hamish went on to have a very successful career at the Firm.

This story shows that, in a meritocratic organization at least, you can assert your equality until shown otherwise—until someone tells you, "No, you have to do what I tell you." You'll find it's rare for that to happen. As Hamish said:

> It sounds extreme, but in a way, to be a successful consultant, you have to assert yourself. Very often, you'll be in a situation where you just have to assume that you can do something, or talk to someone, or get access to some bit of information, even though you may not have the explicit authority to do so.

This is a risky strategy, and the more hierarchical an organization, the riskier it becomes. In a more rigid organization, be more sensitive of where the limits to others' authority lie. And be ready to back down quickly; otherwise, someone will stomp on you.

7

DOING RESEARCH

ABOUT RESEARCH AT McKINSEY

The McKinsey problem-solving process begins with research. Before a team can construct an initial hypothesis, before it can disaggregate a problem into its components and uncover the key drivers, it has to have information.

At the start of a McKinsey-ite's career, most of his time is spent gathering data, whether from one of the Firm's libraries, from McKinsey's many databases, or from the Internet. Gathering, filtering, and analyzing data is the skill exercised most by new associates.

As a result, McKinsey-ites have learned a number of tricks for jump-starting their research. You can use these tricks to find the answers to your business problem too.

DON'T REINVENT THE WHEEL (PART 2)

Whatever the problem, chances are that someone, some-
where, has worked on something similar. Maybe that person
is in your organization and can answer all your questions in
the course of a phone call. Maybe other people in your field,
in another division or another company, have seen the same
problem already—find out who they are and get to know
them. Do your research and ask questions; you will save
yourself a lot of time and effort. Your time is valuable, so
don't waste it by reinventing the wheel!

McKinsey keeps an electronic database called PDNet* containing
reports from recent engagements and internal research. When I
was a first-year associate, one of my jobs at the start of an
engagement was to search PDNet for anything that would shed
light on our current project: comparable industries, comparable
problems. Inevitably, any PDNet query produced a mountain of
documents that I then had to wade through to find the few that
might be relevant. Still, this long day's (and, as often as not,
night's) work usually yielded something to point us in the
right direction.

McKinsey has other resources that help its consultants work
smarter, not harder. These include an excellent business library
that holds every business book or magazine you care to mention;
it also has access to all the major commercial databases such as
Lexis/Nexis, Dun & Bradstreet, Datastream, and the Internet.
Most important, the library has a dedicated staff of information

---

*An electronic database of all PD (practice development) work done by the Firm. It includes
internal research as well as findings from previous client work. For purposes of confidentiality, the Firm disguises client names and data before storing anything on the system.

specialists who work extremely hard to supply the consultants with information—whether from PDNet, the library, or any other source. The Firm also has a cadre of senior information specialists who are experts in particular industries; they were an especially valuable resource when we found ourselves working one month for a client in banking and the next for a jet engine manufacturer.

In my first McKinsey engagement after joining the Firm, our client, the financial arm of a very large computer hardware and software manufacturer, wanted advice on expanding internationally. The client especially wanted to understand how major foreign conglomerates maintained financial and managerial control of their offshore subsidiaries and what the pros and cons of their various methods were. My engagement manager put me in charge of that part of the project. I had three weeks to gain an intimate understanding of four of the world's largest conglomerates and to figure out what, if anything, our client could learn from them.

I went to PDNet first. Fortunately for me, another McKinsey team had recently put together an organizational profile of one of the most complex of my subjects, Daimler-Benz. That afternoon I had in my hands what would have taken me a week's concentrated research; more important, I learned the names of the real experts on Daimler-Benz, whom I called with follow-up questions. I had that much more time to work on the other companies, and the team was able to produce a document that impressed our client.

You may not have PDNet, but if you work in a large organization you probably have access to much of your company's "corporate memory"—databases, files, training manuals, and coworkers. Even if you're on your own, there is a huge stream of information out there for you to take advantage of—trade magazines, newspapers, data feeds, and (most important these days) the Internet. What about your local library? You will find loads of information and valuable resources there with a few hours' digging.

Get to know your competitors. Many businesspeople will share some information on the principle that "what goes around, comes around." If you're in, say, advertising, find the café in your city where other ad execs hang out. Tap into your industry's "buzz."

Whatever you're doing, chances are someone, somewhere has done something similar. Learn from others' successes and mistakes. Leverage your valuable time and don't reinvent the wheel!

SPECIFIC RESEARCH TIPS

Use these tried-and-tested tips to jump-start your research.

During my research for this book, I interviewed dozens of former McKinsey-ites. They gave me, along with structured answers to my specific questions, a number of tips and tricks to succeed in the various aspects of life at McKinsey. Here is a grab bag of tips to make your research more efficient and effective.

Start with the annual report. If you want to get up to speed on a company as quickly as possible, the first place to turn is the annual report. It's easy to obtain (many companies now post their annuals on the World Wide Web) and contains a great deal of information beyond the financial data.

When you get a company's annual, turn first to the "Message to Shareholders" or "Chairman's Remarks" at the front. If you read the section carefully, and a little skeptically, you'll find out a lot about how the company has performed in the last year, where management hopes to take the company in the future, and the strategy for getting there. You'll usually also get a quick breakdown of key financial indicators such as stock price, revenue, and earnings per share. Go further into the annual, and you'll find out about the company's business units and product lines, who its senior managers are, and where the company has offices and production facilities. Then you can plough into the numbers.

A company's annual report will get your research off to a rapid start.

Look for outliers. When you've collected a large amount of data on a particular aspect of your problem, look for outliers—things that are especially good or bad. Use a computer to get a quick picture.

For example, suppose you are collecting data on your company's sales force. Enter the average sales of each salesperson and divide it by the number of accounts served by that salesperson for, say, the last three years; this gives you the average sales per account. Type the data into your favorite spreadsheet software and sort the averages from lowest to highest. Then look at the two or three best and worst figures. Congratulations, you've just found a fruitful area for research. Figure out why the numbers are so good or bad and you'll be well on your way to fixing the problem.

Look for best practice. There's an old saying that no matter how good you are at something, there's always somebody better. This is as true in business as it is anywhere else. Find out what the best performers in the industry are doing and imitate them. Often, this is the quickest antidote to poor performance.

Usually, you can't find out about best practice in the library. You have to think creatively. If some of your competitors have best practice, they probably won't tell you their secrets. Talk to other people in the industry: suppliers, customers, Wall Street analysts, friends from business school, and so forth.

Sometimes you can find best practice within your company. Someone, some team, or some division is outperforming the rest of the company. Find out why. Figure out how to implement the top performer's secrets throughout your organization. The result will be a huge payoff to your business.

8

CONDUCTING INTERVIEWS

ABOUT INTERVIEWING AT McKINSEY

In every McKinsey engagement, someone on the team will conduct an interview. In most engagements, the team will conduct lots of them. There is always someone who has information that the team needs: an executive at the client, a production-line supervisor, a supplier, a customer, an industry expert, even a competitor. Interviewing is the way McKinsey consultants fill the gaps in their knowledge base and tap into the experience and knowledge of their clients.

Interviewing is such an important part of the McKinsey problem-solving process that it merits its own chapter in this book, separate from research. You can learn a lot from reading magazine articles, books, and scholarly papers, but to get the nitty-gritty on an organization, you have to ask questions of and get answers from the people on the front line. Interviewing is a skill in its own right, and most people have no idea how to go about it.

You might think that even though interviewing McKinsey-style is a good technique for consultants who need to get up to speed on unfamiliar industries, it is of little use to executives in more settled positions. I disagree. In today's business world, no matter who you are, from the most junior of junior managers to the most senior of senior vice presidents, you may find yourself in a situation where you need the information in someone else's head. You might be assigned to a multifunctional team as part of a merger; you might be told to set up and run a new business. The possibilities are endless, but they all require you to pick someone's brain, chew the fat, or get up to speed. Call it what you like, it's an interview when you ask questions and get answers.

In this chapter, I will take you through the interviewing process, from preparing your interview guide to writing your thank-you note. If you read no other chapter of the book from start to finish, read this one. I think you'll learn something very valuable that you won't find elsewhere.

BE PREPARED: WRITE AN INTERVIEW GUIDE

When you go into an interview, be prepared. You may have only 30 minutes with a person whom you may never see again. Know what you're going to ask.

When I asked McKinsey alumni for their best advice on interviews, every single one of them said, "Write an interview guide." Many people resent being interviewed, or at least begrudge you the time that you are taking from their day. A guide is your best tool for getting what you want from interviewees and for making the best use of your time—and theirs.

You must think on two levels when constructing your guide. First, and obviously, what are the questions to which you need answers? Write them all down in any order. Second, and more important, what do you really need from this interview? What are you trying to achieve? Why are you talking to this person? Defining your purpose will help you put your questions in the right order and phrase them correctly.

It helps to know as much as possible about the interviewee in advance. Is she a prickly CEO who might bite your head off if you ask a sensitive question? Or is she a middle-level manager whose pleas for change in her organization have gone unheeded? Both might know the same piece of information, but you'd approach each one differently.

At McKinsey we were taught that, as a rule, an interview should start with general questions and move on to specific ones. Don't dive right into a sensitive area like "What are your responsibilities?" or "How long have you been with the company?" Start with anodyne questions about, say, the industry overall.

This will help the interviewee "warm up" and allow you to develop rapport.

When deciding on which questions to ask, you might want to include some to which you know the answer. This may sound counterintuitive, but it's really very useful. On questions of fact, asking a "ringer" will give you some insights into the interviewee's honesty and/or knowledge. For complex issues, you may think you "know" the answer, but there may be more than one; you should find out as many as possible.

Once you've written your guide, look at it and ask yourself, "What are the three things I most want to know by the end of the interview?" These are the things you will focus on when you go into the interviewee's office, the three things that you will try your hardest to obtain before you leave. Sometimes you won't even get those answers (see "Difficult Interviews" later in the chapter), and sometimes they'll come easily. Anything more is gravy.

Finally, every interview guide should conclude with what I call the prototypical McKinsey question. When you've asked all your questions, or you're running out of time, put away your guide and ask the interviewee if there's anything else he'd like to tell you or any question you forgot to ask. As often as not, the interviewee will say no, but every once in a while you'll strike paydirt. Remember that, chances are, the people you interview know their organizations, their business units, or their departments better than you do. They may know which problems are eluding senior managers, who's pushing which agenda, or where the bones are buried. And sometimes, if you're lucky, they'll tell you.

WHEN CONDUCTING INTERVIEWS, LISTEN AND GUIDE

When you're picking people's brains, ask questions and then let them do the talking. Most people like to talk, especially if you let them know you're interested in what they're saying. Keep the interview on track by breaking in when necessary.

McKinsey consultants receive a lot of training in interviewing techniques. The first thing we were taught was "always let the interviewee know you are listening." We did this by filling the gaps in the interviewee's conversation with verbal placeholders such as "yes, or "I see," and even just "uh-huh" (this particular choice I like to call the McKinsey grunt*). Uh-huh may not seem like much, but it shows that you're paying attention (even when you're not!), and it gives the other person a chance to gather his thoughts and catch his breath.

We also learned to communicate our interest through body language. When the interviewee was speaking, we leaned toward her slightly. When she completed a sentence, we nodded. And we always took notes. Even if the interviewee was babbling (and this happened often enough), we had our notepads and pens out and wrote things down. Like the McKinsey grunt, note taking implied we were paying attention and kept us prepared in case the interviewee did say something important.

This technique could be carried too far, of course. According to one piece of Firm lore, two consultants went to interview a

---

*I believe the McKinsey grunt has its origins in Japan. A conversation in Japanese is full of verbal placeholders such as *hai* (yes), *un* (a less polite form of yes) and *so desu ka* (really?). The Japanese even have a word for this: *aizuchi*, which refers to two swordsmiths hammering the same blade in turns.

high-level executive at a client. The engagement manager made his introduction, then started asking questions. The executive answered in detail. All through this, the associate nodded and interjected with "yes," "uh-huh," and "I see" while taking notes at a furious pace, just as he had been taught, but he never asked any questions himself. The EM asked follow-up questions and the associate just kept on nodding and saying "uh-huh." When the interview ended, the EM thanked the executive for his time and the two consultants got up to leave. As they were shaking hands, the executive pointed to the associate and asked the EM, "Does he speak English?"

When McKinsey consultants conduct interviews, it's because they wants access to the information, experience, and anecdotes in other person's heads. Consultants are there to listen, not to talk. They need to remember that the other person has a separate agenda, and needs to be kept on track. The process can sometimes prove difficult. I once had to interview a purchasing manager from a client's plant in Idaho. He knew all about the plant's suppliers, customers, input requirements, and manufacturing processes, but all he cared about was fishing—fly fishing. "Did I fly fish?" he wanted to know. I should try it. If I was ever in the Pocatello area, he could set me up. You get the picture. I felt a bit bad getting him off his favorite subject, but I was there to get information, not swap fish stories.

The main thing to remember when trying to get information from other is that they need to feel you are listening and that you're interested in what they have to say. Use positive body language and always take notes. One final trick: If you want people to say more than they have, if you think they have left out something important but you're not sure what it is, say nothing. Let the silence hang. Nature abhors a vacuum, and so do most people. Chances are they will start talking, just to fill the gap. If they have been giving you a prepared "script," they will probably drop it, because the one thing they were not prepared for was silence. Try it and see. It's surprisingly effective.

SEVEN TIPS FOR SUCCESSFUL INTERVIEWING

Always think strategically when conducting an interview. You have a goal to reach and limited time to reach it. Here are seven tried-and-tested stratagems to help you get what you want from an interviewee.

1. Have the interviewee's boss set up the meeting. Going through the boss tells the interviewee that the interview is important. He'll be less likely to jerk you around if he knows his boss wants him to talk to you.

2. Interview in pairs. It's very difficult to conduct an effective interview on your own. You may be so busy taking notes that it becomes difficult to ask the right questions. You may miss non-verbal clues that the interviewee is giving. Sometimes, it is useful for a pair of interviewers to "tag-team"—switch roles from question poser to note taker during the session. The approach is especially effective when one of the interviewers has specific knowledge on certain issues that will be covered. Furthermore, it is always useful to have two different views of what actually happened in the interview. Just make sure that whoever writes up the interview notes corroborates them with the other interviewer.

3. Listen; don't lead. In most interviews, you are not looking for yes-or-no answers to your questions. You want exhaustive answers—as much information as possible. The way to get them is to listen. Talk as little as possible, just enough to keep the interview on track. Remember that the interviewee probably knows a lot more about her business than you do, and most of the information she gives you will be useful one way or another.

Here's another trick for keeping the information flowing. Ask open-ended questions. If you ask yes-or-no or multiple-choice questions, that's all you will get. For example, suppose you want to find out when a store's busiest season is. You think it is either summer or winter, but you're not sure. If you ask the store manager, "Is your busiest season summer or winter?" she might say summer; she might say winter; or she might say, "Actually, it's spring," in which case, you've just highlighted your lack of knowledge about her business. If you ask her, "What is your busiest season?" she will give you the answer, and probably in more detail than if you gave her multiple choice—for example, "We're busiest in the spring, specifically at Easter." By asking the open-ended question, you get a much better result.

4. Paraphrase, paraphrase, paraphrase. Before going out on interviews, every McKinsey consultant is trained to repeat back a subject's answers in slightly different form. I cannot overstress how important this is. Most people do not think or speak in a completely structured way. They ramble, they digress, they jumble important facts among irrelevancies. If you repeat their own words back to them—ideally with some structure applied—then they can tell you whether you understood them correctly. Paraphrasing also gives the interviewee a chance to add information or amplify important points.

5. Use the indirect approach. An EM had on his team a new associate, fresh out of the Navy. The two had put together a very clear interview guide and had agreed on a specific set of goals for an interview with a middle-level manager at their client, so the EM let the associate take the lead. The associate proceeded to grill the manager aggressively in order to get precisely what he wanted, as if it were an interrogation rather than an interview. As you might imagine, the interviewee was rattled; he became defensive and essentially refused to cooperate.

The moral of this tale is "Be sensitive to the interviewee's feelings." Understand that the person may feel threatened. Don't dive right into the tough questions. If you have to dance around the important issues for a few minutes, that's OK. Take time to make the interviewee comfortable with you and the interview process (for an in-depth discussion, see the next section).

6. Don't ask for too much. There are two reasons not to ask for everything the interviewee has. First, you might get it. When you write your interview guide, you narrow down your goals to the two or three most important questions. If you then ask the interviewee for the sum total of his knowledge of the widget industry, you may find yourself wading through a lot of information to get what you really need, if you even find it at all.

Second, you want to stop short of the straw that breaks the camel's back. Remember, being interviewed, especially in the context of a business problem, is an uncomfortable experience for many. If you compound that discomfort by pressing too hard, you may find that the interviewee becomes uncooperative or even hostile. You never know when you may want to come back to this person for more information, so don't shut the door.

7. Adopt the Columbo tactic. If you watched TV in the 1970s, you may remember Peter Falk's trenchcoat wearing detective, Lieutenant Columbo. After he finished quizzing a murder suspect about her whereabouts on the night in question, he would pick up his rumpled raincoat and head out the door. As he reached the threshold and was about to leave, he would turn around, stick his finger up to his temple, and say, "Excuse me, ma'am, but there's something I forgot to ask." This question invariably gave Columbo the answer he needed to figure out who did it.

If there's a particular question you need the answer to, or a piece of data that you want, the Columbo tactic is often a good way to get it. Once the interview is over, everybody becomes more relaxed. The interviewee's sense that you have some power over him will have disappeared. He is far less likely to be defensive, and will often tell you what you need or give you the information you seek on the spot. Try it; it works.

You might also want to try the "super-Columbo" tactic. Instead of turning around at the door, wait until a day or two has passed, then drop by the interviewee's office. You were just passing by and remembered a question you forgot to ask. Again, this makes you much less threatening, and makes it more likely that you will get the information you need.

DON'T LEAVE THE INTERVIEWEE NAKED

Remember that, for many people, being interviewed about problems in their job or business can be unnerving. You have a responsibility to be sensitive to their fears. It's not only the right thing to do; it makes good business sense too.

A McKinsey associate and his ED went to interview a middle-level manager at a large pharmaceuticals company that the Firm was helping to restructure. The man had been with the company for 20 years; now he was terrified that McKinsey would get him fired. When the consultants came into his office, he was sweating bullets. After introductions were made, he asked the consultants if they would like some coffee; he had a Mr. Coffee on his credenza. He went to pick up the pot to pour, but he couldn't; his hands were shaking too much. He put the pot down and tried again—still no good. Finally, he had to place the rim of the cup hard against the brim of the pot to get the coffee out.

I offer this story to show just how unsettling an interview can be. As the interviewer, someone who is investigating a business problem, you carry power and authority. Not over a CEO or a top-level manager perhaps, but over many others. Imagine what you represent to, say, a store manager whose boss told her to talk to you and who knows there are problems in her organization. I believe you have a professional responsibility to respect the interviewee's anxiety, to allay it, and not to take advantage of it.

Respecting the interviewee's anxiety means not leaving him feeling naked at the end of the interview, as if he's been the subject of a military interrogation. Remember that you're looking for just two or three things in any interview. You shouldn't need to squeeze an interviewee dry to get them. Also, be circumspect about asking questions that, though perfectly appropriate in a business context, may touch on deeply personal matters from the interviewee's perspective. For example, your first question should probably not be "So, what is it that you do, exactly?"

Allaying the fears of interviewees means demonstrating how the process benefits them—not just the interview, but the whole process of solving the organization's problems. If you make their job more efficient, that should benefit them. Likewise, if you improve the profitability of their employer, that might work to their advantage too. Don't be afraid to offer a quid pro quo. Interviewees are giving you information; if you have information that you can share with them, do so. Most people would rather know more about what is going on in their organization.

Not taking advantage of the interviewee's fears means resisting the temptation to use the power of the interview as a blunt instrument. Most of the time, an interviewee is willing to help.

There is no need, in the first instance, to flash your authority like a police badge. If you do that, you may find that, like a gangster in an old cops and robbers movie, the interviewee "clams up." If you run into real obstruction or hostility (see the next section), you may have to bring your authority into play, but not until then. Along with power comes the responsibility to use it wisely.

DIFFICULT INTERVIEWS

Conduct enough interviews and you will encounter difficult ones. Some of them are easy enough to handle, once you know how. Others will test your strength and spirit.

A major New York brokerage house, worried that it was lagging its rivals in profitability, called in McKinsey to do a complete review of its many businesses. The stakes for the company and its executives were high; the prospect of mass firings loomed. The various players in the organization squared off into pro- and anti-McKinsey camps and promoted their agendas vigorously.

Hamish McDermott, a newly promoted EM, had scheduled a meeting with one of the broker's senior managers and his management team. He walked into the man's office and introduced himself. The man replied, "Hamish McDermott, eh? You're the _____ that's been telling the board I've been refusing to meet my cost reduction target."

Sometime in your career, if you aggressively pursue solutions to business problems, you will run into a situation like Hamish's. How do you handle this kind of outright hostility in an interviewee? Here's how Hamish did it:

His words were pretty shocking to me, especially since they weren't true. But I didn't get angry and I didn't back down. I simply explained that I thought he was mistaken and said that we still had to have our meeting.

He did it partly because he was a difficult guy and partly to see if we would back down. If someone says something blatantly false like that, you have to challenge him; you can't back down.

This strategy worked very well for us. Afterwards several of his staff came and apologized that we had been insulted in this way. They thought we had handled it with a great deal of dignity and strength; we established credibility with a number of important people in the organization, and that helped us later on.

The limits to this strategy are the limits of your authority in the organization. McKinsey consultants usually have the backing of the top management at the client and can thus stand up to anyone. If you aren't so favored, just remember that if the person you are interviewing is more senior than the person who authorized your project, you will probably have to back down when challenged.

A less hostile, but equally difficult situation arises when interviewees refuse to give you information. They won't answer your question or give you access to relevant documents or data. When this happens, it is time to "pull rank." If you're there asking them questions, then someone in your organization (or your client) wants you to be there. Let them know that. If they still refuse, play hardball. If necessary, call the boss on the phone there and then. You probably won't have to; just the suggestion should open the information floodgates. You're not in the schoolyard any longer; no one will call you a tattletale.

You may also encounter difficulty when interviewing what psy-chiatrists might call the passive-aggressive type, but I like to call "the Sandbagger." Sandbaggers will talk all you want; they just won't tell you anything, as one former McKinsey EM found out:

> I walked into this woman's office—we had blocked out an hour for the interview—and she told me that she could give me only half an hour. She then proceeded to talk for the next 30 minutes about what *she* thought McKinsey did and why it was that McKinsey was there. When she ran out of steam on that topic, she told me the story of her life. I couldn't get a word in edgewise.

Handling a Sandbagger requires an indirect approach. Often the most useful strategy is finding someone else in the organization who can tell you what you want to know. If the Sandbagger is the only source for the information, then you may have to ask her boss to have a quiet word with her.

The last category of difficult interview is also the hardest to handle. I can think of few more stressful situations than being face to face with someone who knows your work will likely get him fired—and you know it too. Unfortunately, there is very little you can do in such cases apart from playing the "good soldier." You have to do your job, and you have to get the interviewee to help you. It's for the good of the organization. You can't become angry or upset, despite the unfairness of it all. In a way, there is no effec-tive strategy. You just have to reach down inside yourself and push on through. No one ever said life was fair.

ALWAYS WRITE A THANK-YOU NOTE

When you get back to your office after interviewing some-one, take the time to write a thank-you letter. It's polite and professional, and could pay you back in unexpected ways.

If your mother was like my mother, then when you were a kid you were always told to write a thank-you note after you received a gift. I have a large extended family, so after holidays and birth-days I spent what seemed like weeks writing letters to aunts and uncles and second cousins thanking them for whatever it was they had sent me, whether I liked it or not. My mom would always be after me, making sure I wrote those thank-you notes (as well as reading them and checking my penmanship). I didn't realize it then, but this proved good training for my time at the Firm.

After you've taken half an hour or more out of someone's day to interview and get information from him, you should take the time to thank him in writing. As my mom could tell you, it's polite. It shows that you value the interviewee's time as much as he does. It's also professional. Sending someone a few choice words below your corporate letterhead puts your company in a favorable light.

My mom taught me to avoid boilerplate thank-you notes. "Dear _____, thank you for the _____. I will always cherish it" was unacceptable when I was a boy. It's still unacceptable today. That doesn't mean each thank-you note you write needs to be a gem of immaculately crafted prose. Just make sure it doesn't read like a computer-generated form letter. I keep the text of a basic thank-you note on my hard drive; when I need to write one, I alter it to suit each particular recipient. It takes a few extra seconds, but it's worth it. It's also much easier than it was when I was 13, and had to write all those thank-you notes by hand.

Sometimes a thank-you note can yield an unexpected payoff. Every new McKinsey-ite hears the story of the associate who needs to interview a senior sales executive at an agricultural products company somewhere in America's heartland. When he calls the man saying he's from McKinsey and would like an hour of his time, he receives an effusive welcome from the other end of the line. "Come on down," he is told. When the associate arrives after a long journey, the man shows him a letter on McKinsey stationery, from another McKinsey associate, thanking the executive for his time on a day 15 years in the past. The letter has pride of place on the man's office wall, along with his college diploma, hanging in a frame.

Sometimes a little politeness goes a long way.

9

BRAINSTORMING

ABOUT BRAINSTORMING AT McKINSEY

When the study has been sold, the team assembled, and the preliminary research done, the real work can begin. Brainstorming is the sine qua non of strategic consulting. It's what the clients really buy. Let's face it. Most large, modern corporations are chock full of intelligent, knowledgeable managers who are darned good at day-to-day problem solving. McKinsey offers a new mindset, an outsider's view that is not locked into "the company way" of doing things. That's what clients need when problems cannot be solved within the organization, and it starts in a meeting room with a table, some chairs, a bunch of pads, pens and pencils, some markers, and a clean "white board."

Before the first brainstorming session, McKinsey consultants do their homework. Everyone on the team reads the results of the PDNet and library searches. The associates put together and distribute "fact packs" based on their preliminary research. The ED, the EM, and possibly the more senior associates on the team come up with initial hypotheses that the team will then test to destruction.

Brainstorming takes time. Typically, a McKinsey team blocks out two hours, if not more, for a brainstorming session. Some team leaders prefer weekends for their meetings, though this is not always looked on favorably by the other members of the team. These sessions often run well into the night, fueled by deliveries of pizza, Chinese food, or sushi (my personal favorite). I even recall some teams bringing in a six-pack or two of beer for a weekend session (presumably to stimulate the flow of ideas). McKinsey's U.S. offices keep "menu books" of the favored local food delivery services; these books see a lot of use.

The most important ingredient for successful brainstorming is a clean slate. There's no point calling a meeting if you're just going to look at the data in the same old way. You have to leave your preconceptions and prejudices at the door of the meeting room. That way, you are free to manipulate the facts in your mind.

I like to think of brainstorming as playing with that old puzzle Rubik's Cube. Each fact is a face on one of the small cubes. Turn the faces this way and that, and you'll come up with the answer, or at least *an* answer.

Another metaphor I like to use is shuffling a pack of cards. Each fact is a card. When you first open the pack, all the cards are in order. How boring. Shuffle the cards, or throw them into the air and see how they land. Now you might find some interesting patterns: straights, flushes, full houses. The same thing happens when you toss around facts and ideas.

In the next few lessons, we'll take a closer look at the various aspects of brainstorming à la McKinsey, and learn a few tips to make your brainstorming more productive.

PROPER PRIOR PREPARATION

Although brainstorming has an airy-fairy, college bull session connotation to some, in reality effective brainstorming requires some hard-nosed advance work.

The cardinal rule of brainstorming is that you cannot do it successfully in a vacuum. Before you go into that meeting, you have to know something about the problem you'll be working on. Don't just stride into the meeting expecting to wow everyone with your brilliance. As with all things McKinsey, there is a method to preparing for your brainstorming session, whether you are the leader (or, as some prefer, moderator or facilitator) or just a participant.

If you have followed the outline of Part Two sequentially—that is, you've completed your research—then half your preparation is done already. Now make sure that everyone on the team knows what you know. Put your research into what McKinsey-ites call a "fact pack," a neatly organized summary of the key points and data that you've discovered, and circulate it to your team. If you are the leader, make sure that all your team members put their research into fact packs. Making a fact pack is easy. It doesn't require a detailed structure, just a little thought about what is important and how to show it. Once everyone on the team has read all the fact packs, you'll all have the same knowledge base when it comes time to generate ideas.

Once you have absorbed your team's fact base, what next? McKinsey-ites fall into two camps on this subject. The first group says, "Familiarize yourself with the outlines of the problem and the data. Don't try to come up with an answer before the session starts." The counterproposition states, "Always come in with a hypothesis; otherwise, you waste too much time flailing around looking for ideas." I come down firmly between these two assertions—they're both right. If you can come up with a hypothesis, fine; if you're the team leader, you probably ought to have one. Just don't march into the team room saying, "This is the answer." The right attitude is, "I think this may be how things are. Let's attack this hypothesis as a group."

You can also prepare by brainstorming on your own, ahead of time. Rather than come up with a single hypothesis, get an idea of the likely *set* of hypotheses that your team will come up with—the solutions that fit within the scope of your project. You can then quickly dismiss hypotheses that are unrealistic, while giving your team free rein to work on ideas that are more plausible. This approach keeps your brainstorming grounded in reality, which, as one former McKinsey director observed, is all that is out there.

However you go about it, just make sure that, at the very least, you know the facts. Remember the Boy Scout motto: "Be prepared."

IN A WHITE ROOM

The point of brainstorming is the generation of new ideas. So start with tabula rasa—*a clean slate. When you get your team into the room, leave your preconceptions at the door. Bring the facts you know, but find new ways of looking at them.*

In the last section, I suggested that you spend a few hours on your own, knocking around the facts and devising a set of hypotheses. Now I'm going to recommend that you come into the brainstorming meeting without any preconceptions. If that seems contradictory to you, well brainstorming benefits from a few contradictions—provided they help stimulate your thinking.

Again, brainstorming is about generating *new* ideas. If all the team members come into the room saying the same old things and agreeing with one another, then you've gained nothing and wasted time. Even worse, if the team leader comes in and imposes her view on everyone else, the team has missed an opportunity to achieve a solution that's more creative and, possibly, better.

Brainstorming requires the participation of everyone in the room, from the most senior director to the most junior analyst—and there's no guarantee on any given day that the former will have better ideas than the latter. No one should be afraid to speak his mind in the brainstorming room. So, along with your preconceptions, check your hierarchy and deference at the door.

Here's an example of how *not* to run a brainstorming session. When Kristin Asleson was a new associate, the SEM on her engagement called the team members in for a brainstorming session. When they got there, the SEM said, "Just be quiet and watch me work through the problem on the white board." They then sat there for the next hour watching the SEM think to himself. It may have been instructive, but it wasn't brainstorming, unless it was brainstorming as theater.

Here are a few more "rules of the road" for successful brainstorming.

There are no bad ideas. No one should ever hesitate to open her mouth during a brainstorming session for fear of getting zinged with the words "That's a bad idea." If the idea was sincerely meant, but you disagree with it, take a minute to explain why. Debating ideas is part of the brainstorming process. Who knows? After a few minutes of discussion it, it might not seem such a bad idea after all. At least give it a chance. Obviously, ideas that are not directed at the problem at hand don't count—for example, "Let's forget about the problem and go play Frisbee" (unless you think the team might benefit from a quick game).

There are no dumb questions. Just as there are no bad ideas, any question should be taken on its merits. Never be afraid to ask why something is the way it is or is done the way it's done. Often the answer is "Well, gee, that's the way we've always done it"— which is not a good reason to do much of anything.

Never discount the benefits of working through seemingly obvious or simple questions. For example, when I was working on an engagement for a money management company, at our first brainstorming meeting, the brand-new associate on our team asked, "How much money is there in the world?" Rather than just saying "lots," we spent the next 45 minutes thinking through the dynamics of international money management and came out with some useful insights.

Be prepared to kill your babies. This rather shocking notion originated among Hollywood screenwriters. It means that if your idea, no matter how good, is not part of the team's answer at the end of the session, dispense with it. Look upon your hypothesis as just one more datum to throw into the brainstorming mix. Offer it up to your teammates and let them knock it around. It may be "right" or it may be "wrong," but the main thing is that it should help the team think through the problem at hand. Don't invest a lot of your ego in your hypothesis; don't come to the meeting prepared to die in a ditch defending it.

Know when to say when. Brainstorming takes time, but if you stay at it too long, you'll hit the point of rapidly diminishing returns. The consensus among former McKinsey-ites is that a team can stand about two hours of brainstorming before the atmosphere deteriorates. In my opinion, this time frame is especially true of evening sessions. Unless the team is composed completely of night owls, people become tired, cranky, and slow off the mark as the night wears on. There are always exceptions, of course. Sometimes you get on a roll and the adrenaline keeps you productive until well past midnight. Sometimes you gain insight by contemplating your colleague's plate of leftover fried rice. In general, though, it's best to call a halt before the team starts coasting. There's always the next day, or the weekend.

If you must hold an all-day session, you have to make allowances to keep the participants' energy level up. Let conversations go on tangents; allow people to make jokes and let off steam, but rein them in after a little while to keep them focused. Take breaks every now and then—and not just for lunch, dinner, and calls of nature. If you can take a half-hour walk somewhere, do so. It's a great opportunity for people to gather their thoughts and stretch their legs.

Get it down on paper. Unlike a regular meeting, where someone has the job of taking minutes, brainstorming doesn't lend itself to precise note taking. Ideas flit around the room like mayflies and can die just as quickly. You cannot, under any circumstances, leave the room and turn off the lights without a permanent record of the outcome. Don't think that, in the rush of coming up with a brilliant idea, you'll never forget it. Once the adrenaline wears off and fatigue sets in, you will.

McKinsey uses an excellent device to preserve the outcomes of brainstorming sessions. Although practically every meeting room has a white board and markers that wipe clean with an eraser or paper towel, some have white boards that can make paper copies of whatever is written on them. It's an excellent way to get the final copy of that brilliant idea or killer chart you sketched at 2 a.m.

You can duplicate this high-tech marvel with low-tech flipcharts. The only drawback to flipcharts is that marker ink on paper doesn't erase—so be neat. At the end of the meeting, give someone the job of transcribing all the flipcharts onto regular paper and circulating copies to the team.

SOME BRAINSTORMING EXERCISES

The key to successful brainstorming is good preparation and a proper frame of mind. Here are a few tricks that McKinsey-ites use to get the maximum benefit from their brainstorming sessions.

While Kristin Asleson was at the Firm, she took part in an experimental training program on brainstorming, during which she learned the following exercises. They can help you get your brainstorming seminar off to a good start.

The Post-it™ exercise. Give everyone in the room a pad of sticky notes. The participants then write out any relevant ideas they have, one idea per note, and hand them over to the leader, who reads them aloud. This is a very good way to generate a lot of ideas quickly without getting bogged down in discussing each one as it comes out.

The flipchart exercise. Put a number of flipcharts around the room, each one labeled with a different category or issue. Each team member then goes around the room writing ideas down on the appropriate flipchart. If you like, you can give each team member a different colored marker, so you know whose ideas are whose.

Bellyaches up front. Kristin remembers a particularly effective method for handling large-scale brainstorming meetings in a tense atmosphere:

We invited all the relevant players into a large room to discuss options for change at the client. We asked them to tell us up front everything they didn't like about the program we had presented. Once they had vented, we asked them to come up with things that were good about it, and ways that it could be implemented within their own business units—this required some "tough love" from our ED. The technique worked in two ways: It yielded some excellent ideas that we would not have otherwise come up with; and it helped a previously skeptical, if not outright hostile, management team buy into McKinsey's solution.

One more tip for handling a grumbler or rabble-rouser at a brainstorming session: Have the leader or moderator stand behind him, and even touch him on the shoulder occasionally. This lets the troublemaker know that he is being watched. If he mutters an aside, the moderator can ask him to speak up, rather like the teacher who tells the note-passing student, "Why don't you share it with the class?"

Try these exercises to jazz up your own brainstorming sessions. You'll be impressed with the results.

THE McKINSEY WAY OF SELLING SOLUTIONS

You've read Parts One and Two. You know how to think about business problems and how to work effectively to come up with practical solutions to them. Now it's time to go forth and conquer the world, right? Not quite. The best solution, no matter how well researched, how thoroughly analyzed, how glitteringly, flawlessly structured, is worth exactly nothing if your clients don't buy into it.

To get your clients to buy into your solution, you have to *sell* it to them. That's what we'll cover in Part Three. You'll learn how to put together a presentation that conveys your ideas to your audience. You'll discover how to manage internal communications so everyone on your team can stay "on message." You'll find out how to work with and manage your client organizations and the people who work in them—the good ones *and* the bad ones. And you'll learn how to take your brilliant solution from paper to real life—how to make change happen.

10

MAKING PRESENTATIONS

ABOUT PRESENTATIONS AT McKINSEY

McKinsey communicates with its clients through presentations. They may be formal presentations: meetings held around boardroom tables with neatly bound blue books. They may be informal presentations between a few managers at the client and a couple of McKinsey consultants with several charts hastily stapled together into a deck. As junior members advance through the ranks at the Firm, they spend a lot of time presenting ideas to other people.

McKinsey has become extremely good at communicating in this way. You can apply many of the Firm's techniques in your own presentations. They will help you get your message across—which, after all, is the goal of the process.

BE STRUCTURED

For your presentation to succeed, it must take the audience down the path of your logic in clear, easy to follow steps.

We went over the structure of the McKinsey problem-solving process at great length in Part One of this book (see "Feel Free to Be MECE" in Chapter 1). The rest of the world sees the McKinsey structure most often through the medium of the Firm's presentations. They are where the rubber meets the road.

A presentation reflects the thinking of the person or team that put it together. If your presentation is sloppy and muddled, your audience will assume that your thinking is also sloppy and muddled—regardless of whether that is the case. So, whatever structure you applied to your thought process, apply it to your presentation. If you use the McKinsey structure, use it in your presentation. If you prefer some other organizing principle, make sure your presentation reflects it—assuming, of course, that your thought process is structured and logical.

Let me reiterate that you do not have to use the McKinsey structure if you are not comfortable with it—if it is not the way you think. A friend of mine at business school became an entrepreneur; like many entrepreneurs, he was capable of brilliant insights and intuitive leaps, but his thinking was not particularly organized. He made many successful presentations using the basic structure of "Tell 'em what you're going to tell 'em, tell 'em, tell 'em what you told 'em." He followed a structure and it worked for him.

Usually, if you adhere to a structure that makes a step-by-step progression, you want the audience to follow your presentation at your pace. There's usually someone in the audience who lacks the patience for this. One McKinsey EM faced the problem of a senior manager at his client who, when handed a presentation document, would invariably leaf through it from beginning to end and then "tune out" for the rest of the meeting. But the EM found a solution. For his team's final presentation, he handed the manager a blue book with all the pages stapled together—no more leafing.

REMEMBER THAT THERE ARE DIMINISHING MARGINAL RETURNS TO EFFORT

Resist the temptation to tweak your presentation right up to the last minute. Weigh the value of a change against a good night's sleep for you and your team. Don't let the best be the enemy of the good.

McKinsey-ites are bound together by a set of common experiences: training programs, interviews, "all-nighters," and more. One of the most common and most unnecessary experiences shared by almost every associate in the Firm is the 4 a.m. vigil in the copier room waiting for the presentation booklets to be put together for tomorrow's (although now it's today's) big progress review. I once spent a pleasant two hours early one morning removing one chart from 40 spiral-bound copies of a blue book and replacing it with a new version, all because of one typo. Another associate and his EM worked through the night cutting and pasting new numbers onto a chart with razor blades and a glue stick (this was before computer graphics became widely available at the Firm).

Many businesspeople and many organizations will accept nothing less than perfection. In many cases, this is laudable: No one wants to ride in an airplane where the engine mounting bolts fit *almost* correctly. However, when you are preparing a presentation, even to the hardest-nosed CEO of the most powerful corporation, don't let the best be the enemy of the good. At some point, usually well before the actual presentation, nitpicking changes no longer add value. Learn to recognize that point and draw the line on changes well in advance of the meeting.

Think about it this way: What matters more, that your team gets a good night's sleep before the presentation or that there is a typo in the final document? Every document of any length will have a few typos, no matter how hard you search and despite spell-checking software (or, sometimes, because of it). On rare occasions, that typo may *have* to be corrected, but only rarely. Far better that you come to the presentation rested, not harried and bedraggled; giving a presentation is stressful enough as it is.

Drawing the line on changes requires discipline. If yours is the final say on the presentation, you just have to discipline yourself. Tell yourself and your team that you want the documents printed, copied, bound, or transferred onto slides—whatever it is that you need—at least 24 hours before the big moment. Spend the time between then and the presentation rehearsing, discussing possible questions that may arise, or just taking a relaxed day at the office, if you can.

If, as is the case for any EM at McKinsey, you put together the presentation but someone senior to you (e.g., your ED) has the final say on the document, then you have to manage upward as strongly as you can. Be firm in telling your boss that she must sign off on the document in time for you to meet your 24-hour deadline. Some senior managers can't resist meddling up to the last moment—you have to resist for them.

PREWIRE EVERYTHING

A good business presentation should contain nothing new for the audience. Walk all the players at the client through your findings before you gather them into one room.

Imagine it is the start of your final presentation. Your findings have been kept confidential to avoid any leaks into the market. You and your team are meeting with the top executives of your company, who are eager finally to hear your recommendations. Your boss is here; your boss's boss is here; the heads of all your company's business units are here; your CEO is sitting at the head of the table hanging on your every word.

You begin to speak. "Ladies and gentlemen," you say, "after weeks of exhaustive research, my team and I have reached the conclusion that the future of our company requires us to increase our investment in widget production by 75 percent over the next two years." As you reach for your first chart of backup analysis, a murmur is heard from the audience. The director of the gadgets division is incensed. Surely, he says, the future of the company lies with gadgets. The CFO protests that the company doesn't have that level of funds available. The president of the widgets subsidiary rushes to your defense. Your moment in the corporate sun dissolves into a shouting match. Clearly, not everyone likes surprises.

To avoid this disaster scenario, McKinsey consultants engage in "prewiring." Before they hold a presentation or progress review, a McKinsey team will take all the relevant players in the client organization through their findings in private. That way, there are few, if any, surprises on the big day. As one former EM said, "It was very rare for us to do a presentation where we hadn't taken the various players through our findings beforehand. Otherwise, it was just too risky. In effect, the actual presentation became performance art."

When prewiring, you must remember the cardinal rule of being a successful consultant or corporate troubleshooter: Not only do you have to come up with the "right" answer; you also have to sell that answer to your client. Sometimes, this just requires salesmanship; other times, it takes compromise. Suppose you walk into the office of Bob, the Director of the Gadgets Division, and tell him that you think the answer is to invest more in widgets, at the expense of gadgets. He is unlikely to be pleased, but when you are alone with him in his office, you are far more likely to be able to take him through your analysis step by step.

By the end of the process, the gadgets director may be convinced (great, move on to the next person) or he may come up with some fact you hadn't known about that alters your recommendation (which does happen, believe me), or he may refuse to accept your recommendation without some changes. In the last case, you have to negotiate. If the compromise is small, make it and move on; if his demands are too great, you will have to figure out a way to bypass him. Of course, if he throws you out of his office (unlikely, but possible), you have a problem on your hands the size of which is in proportion to the director of gadgets' power in the organization.

Let's go back to our scenario at the beginning of this section. This time, though, imagine that you have prewired your presentation with all the senior managers at the table, including the unrelenting director of gadgets. "Ladies and gentlemen," you say, "after weeks of exhaustive research, my team and I have reached the conclusion that the future of our company requires us to increase our investment in widget production by 75 percent over the next two years." As you reach for your first slide, the director of gadgets says, "I've heard this before, and it's horse _____. We have to increase our gadget production." The CFO raises an eyebrow, but says nothing—you've already shown him how he can fund the additional investment. The SVP of the widget subsidiary, secure in the knowledge that she will be the winner at the end of today's presentation, merely looks in the direction of the CEO. The CEO leans back in his chair, steeples his fingers, and tells the gadgets director: "Now come on, Bob, I think we're all pulling on the same oar here. Let's get through the presentation, then we can discuss it at the end." You already know what that outcome will be. Isn't it better to skip the surprise ending?

11

DISPLAYING DATA
WITH CHARTS

ABOUT CHARTS AT McKINSEY

McKinsey relies on charts, graphical representations of information, as a primary means of communicating with its clients. The Firm has devoted a lot of time and effort to discover what works with charts and what does not. You can find most of this wisdom in a book by Gene Zelazny, the Firm's guru of charts and presentations, entitled *Say It With Charts*.* It's an excellent resource and I don't intend to repeat its contents here.

In this chapter, I explain the overarching McKinsey philosophy of charts, and why it will work for you. I also share with you the one McKinsey chart that I have never seen used outside the Firm.

---

*Gene Zelazny, *Say It With Charts: The Executive's Guide to Successful Presentations* (Homewood, IL: Dow-Jones Irwin, 1985).

KEEP IT SIMPLE — ONE MESSAGE PER CHART

The more complex a chart becomes, the less effective it is at conveying information. Use charts as a means of getting your message across, not as an art project.

When I started at the Firm, the first pieces of equipment I was issued were a box of mechanical pencils, an eraser, and a set of ruled, plastic templates with cutouts for various shapes: circles, rectangles, triangles, arrows, and so forth. "Don't lose those templates," I was told. "They're expensive to replace and you'll need them to draw your charts." This was in 1989, hardly the Stone Age, and for years I had been using computer graphics to draw charts and graphs in my previous jobs and at business school. It struck me as slightly primitive: evidence of a corporate culture that was inflexible in the face of advancing technology.

I was partly right, for McKinsey's culture *is* strong and thus slow to change, but I was also partly wrong; those templates served a very important purpose: to keep our charts simple. Computer graphics make it too easy to get fancy. The Firm uses charts as a means of expressing information in a readily understandable form. The simpler things are, the easier they are to understand. Therefore, McKinsey prints its charts in black and white; it avoids three-dimensional graphics unless absolutely necessary to convey the message; and it adheres to the cardinal rule of one message per chart. The first two strictures are visual. The medium must not overpower the message; hence the ban on distracting colors or deceptive 3-D perspectives. The rule of one message per chart affects the way information is interpreted for the audience.

The information in a chart may be highly complex and expressive of multiple points or ideas; the job of the chartist is to pick which point to make. McKinsey consultants do this with the "lead," the caption at the top of the chart. A good lead expresses the point of the chart in one simple sentence (see Figure 11-1). The salient information in the chart may be highlighted, with a different shading, an exploded pie slice, or (as I've done here) with an arrow, among other methods. If a chart offers several insights, copy it with a new lead and the relevant information highlighted (see Figure 11-2).

Also, look in the lower left corner of either chart. You'll see a source attribution. McKinsey charts always include one. Why? So that when people ask, "Where did you get this information?" you

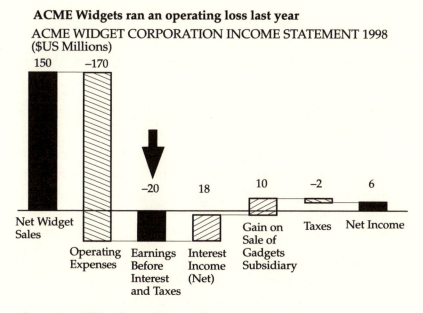

ACME Widgets ran an operating loss last year
ACME WIDGET CORPORATION INCOME STATEMENT 1998 ($US Millions)

Source: Acme Widget Corporation annual report.

Figure 11-1. A good lead highlights the salient information in a chart.

We would have posted a loss in 1998 without the sale of our gadgets divison

ACME WIDGET CORPORATION INCOME STATEMENT 1998 ($US Millions)

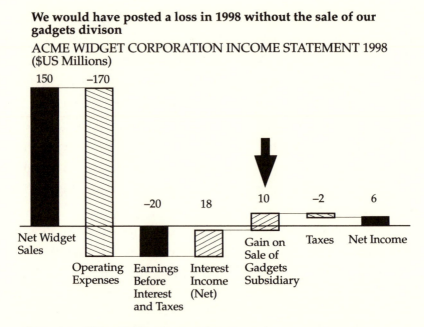

Source: Acme Widget Corporation annual report.

Figure 11-2. A new lead offers different insight into the same information.

can tell them. Also, if at some future time you (or anyone else) want to review the data, you'll know where to look.

One final word about charts: Too many will bore your audience. Use the absolute minimum necessary to make your point, or you may find that your audience hasn't absorbed the last 10 to 15 pages of your presentation.

Time has marched on since 1989, technology has advanced, and McKinsey has learned to live with computer graphics. Associates can now draw their charts in PowerPoint™, and occasionally you'll see a McKinsey chart with a bit of color. But the Firm still adheres to the admirable principle of simplicity.

USE A WATERFALL CHART TO SHOW THE FLOW

The waterfall chart—seldom seen outside McKinsey and not generally available in computer graphics packages—is an excellent way to illustrate quantitative flows.

When you looked at each sample chart in the last section, you probably wondered exactly what type of chart you were seeing. It looked something like a column chart, but not like any you'd find in the chart libraries of Excel™, Freelance™, or any of the other popular computer graphics packages. The chart may have looked strange, but I'll bet you didn't have a lot of trouble understanding it. It's called a waterfall chart, and McKinsey-ites use it all the time, although it's rarely found anywhere else.

When I asked former McKinsey-ites what lessons they learned about charts, one thing they all mentioned was waterfall charts. They loved them, and sometimes used them in their own work, but seldom saw them elsewhere. In my modest ambition to make the world a better place, I herewith offer the secret of the waterfall chart.

The waterfall chart is an excellent method of illustrating how you get from number A to number B. The charts in Figures 11-1 and 11-2 depict a simplified income statement, starting with sales on the left and ending with net income on the right, and show the various items that lead from one to the other. The starting point (sales in the example) is always a column that begins at zero. Positive items such as interest income are depicted as columns that start at the high point of the preceding column and reach upward. Negative items such as operating expenses are columns that start at the high point of the preceding column and extend downward. The total is the distance from the top of the last item (or bottom if that item is negative) to the zero line. Subtotals can be included along the way in the same manner.

Waterfalls can depict static data (balance sheets, income statements) or active data (time series data, cashflows). You can mix negative and positive items (e.g., we started with 6 accounts, gained 3 in the first quarter, then lost 2 in the next quarter, for a total of 7), or you can segregate them to show, say, where value is created and where it is destroyed (e.g., we make money in widgets, gadgets, and thingamajigs; we lose money in flummeries, frankincense, and myrrh).

Whatever data you use, the waterfall chart is a versatile way to convey a lot of information in a clear, concise manner. So go with the flow.

12

MANAGING INTERNAL COMMUNICATIONS

ABOUT INTERNAL COMMUNICATIONS
AT McKINSEY

The success of a team-based operation depends on open communication, both from the top down and from the bottom up. McKinsey has the same methods of internal communication as those available to any modern organization: voice mail, e-mail, memos, meetings, the water fountain, and so forth. It is fair to say that in the area of internal communications the Firm as a whole has no new insights to offer. On the other hand, former McKinsey-ites, in their many combined years of experience, have garnered a number of useful methods for managing internal communications that you can use.

KEEP THE INFORMATION FLOWING

Information is to your team what gasoline is to a car's engine. If you choke off the flow, you'll stall.

Elsewhere in this book, I've mentioned the famous Mushroom Method of management: "Keep them in the dark, cover them with manure, and see what crops up." Most people don't realize that the Mushroom Method can operate in both directions; it is possible to keep your boss in the dark too. No matter which direction the manure is dumped, the Mushroom Method is unproductive. For a successful team operation, you have to keep the information flowing.

Make sure your team is up to date with at least the broad outlines of your project. This is especially true of large undertakings. Being "in the loop" will help your teammates understand how their work is contributing to the final goal, how their efforts are worthwhile. Conversely, when people feel that they are working in a vacuum, that they are alienated from the greater enterprise, their morale is sure to suffer. Also, if you keep your teammates up to date, they'll return the favor. At the ground level, they may be closer to events than you are. Good information flow can help you spot emerging problems (or opportunities) faster.

Always keep your boss up to date with your team's progress. Don't think that your boss will stay out of your way if you keep her in the dark. She'll be far more comfortable when she knows that everything is under control. If things are not under control, then you want your boss to know exactly what the problems are so she can apply her expertise as effectively as possible.

There are two basic methods of internal communication: the

message (whether in the form of voice mail, e-mail, or memo) and the meeting. I'll suggest some tips for successful messages in the next section. Right now, let's concentrate on meetings.

Meetings form the glue that holds your team together. Team meetings allow excellent information flow, in all directions, and provide a certain amount of social bonding. They help remind those present that they are part of a team. Suzanne Tosini, a former McKinsey EM and now a senior manager at Freddie Mac, noted that one of the keys to a successful meeting is making sure everyone attends. To ensure that people do show up, make team meetings a regular item on everybody's schedule. If you have nothing to discuss, then cancel the meeting (as far in advance as possible); your teammates can always find a use for the extra 45 minutes.

Suzanne's other two keys for a successful meeting are an agenda and a leader. Keep the number of items on your agenda to the minimum needed to make sure everyone is up to date with important events, issues, and problems. If something can be put on hold for another time, it probably should. If you are the leader, make sure you cover your agenda as briskly as possible: Frequent meetings are good, unnecessarily long ones are not.

One other method of internal communication is in a class by itself: learning by walking around. Some of the most valuable conversations in my experience resulted from random encounters—in the corridors, at the water cooler, on the way to lunch, at the Firm, or at the client. You can gain a lot just by wandering around and talking to people, and they can learn a lot from you. Never underestimate the value of the random fact.

However you choose to communicate with your team, make sure that you do so frequently and openly. You will boost your team's efficiency and morale, as well as your boss's peace of mind. Turn on the lights and clear out the manure!

THE THREE KEYS TO AN EFFECTIVE MESSAGE

A good business message has three attributes: brevity, thoroughness and structure. Include all three in every voice mail, e-mail or memo you send and you'll get your message across.

A message, whether it's an e-mail, a voice mail, a memo, or a sticky note covered in cramped handwriting, is a presentation in miniature—a means of conveying information to an audience. As such, an effective message shares the same properties as an effective presentation: It is brief, covering *only* the points the audience needs to know; it is thorough, covering *all* the points the audience needs to know; and it has a structure that conveys those points clearly to its audience.

1. Brevity. Brevity, or rather the lack of it, is much more of a problem in spoken than written communications. Many business-people can write concise memos, but how many can record a concise voice mail? To join that select group, think before you speak (or write). Whittle down your message to the three or four points that the audience needs to know. If necessary, write these things down on paper. Some McKinsey-ites write the entire message out like a script before sending a voice mail to their ED or DCS. I think that's going a bit too far—just the bullet points will do.

2. Thoroughness. Make sure your message contains everything your audience needs to know. You are not trying to keep your audience in suspense. Don't just tell your boss, "I'm doing X, Y, and Z. Call me if you have any questions." Tell her not only what you are doing, but what the issues are and what your thoughts are on them. Don't just check in; it's a waste of your boss's time (and yours). If you don't have anything useful to say, wait until you do.

3. Structure. To be readily understood, a message must follow a structure, and that structure must be readily apparent to the audience. Even if you're just writing a one-page e-mail or leaving a 30-second voice message, a simple structure will help your message get through. It can be as basic as this:

We have three problems. In order of increasing importance, they are:

1. Our widgets are too expensive.
2. Our sales force is incompetent.
3. Our widget factory was just destroyed in a freak meteorite impact.

Sometimes McKinsey-ites can take structuring their messages a bit too far. One EM in the New York office was reputed to put her shopping lists in Firm format. Another left affectionate messages on his wife's answering machine—following the McKinsey structure.

Although you needn't follow the extreme examples of these overzealous McKinsey-ites, in your business communications you would do well to remember the three keys to effective messaging.

ALWAYS LOOK OVER YOUR SHOULDER

You cannot be an effective consultant if you don't maintain confidentiality. Know when you can talk and when you can't. Be just a bit paranoid.

During my first week at McKinsey, I went through a short orientation course along with the rest of my Firm "classmates." During a seminar on confidentiality, the EM leading the discussion mentioned that when he stayed over at his girlfriend's apartment, he kept his briefcase locked. At the time, that struck me as a bit extreme. After all, if you can't trust your girlfriend, whom can you trust? (OK, I was young and naïve at the time.) It was only after I had been at the Firm a bit longer that I realized quite how seriously McKinsey takes confidentiality.

McKinsey's corporate culture continually reinforces confidentiality. We always kept it in the back of our minds. If we were on a plane, we didn't take client information out of our briefcases and work on it; we never knew who might be sitting next to us—a competitor, a journalist, maybe even someone from your client. If we needed those three hours to work, it was our tough luck.

We never mentioned our clients by name outside the office, and sometimes not even at the Firm. McKinsey often works for more than one client in an industry, so some information had to be kept even from fellow consultants. We often used code words when discussing our clients, though not always successfully. One EM from Germany recalled coming home to find a note from his girlfriend (who worked for a competing consulting firm) saying that the dinner for Code A (pronounced, in German, as "code ah") would take place at a fancy Munich restaurant. In fact, the name of the client company was Coda; the caller had used the client's real name, although luckily he had been misunderstood. The EM was not pleased.

You may not need to maintain confidentiality while working on your business problem—then again, maybe you do. Ask yourself a few simple questions: What would happen if you were sitting on an airplane and one of your competitors saw what you were working on? How about someone from your company who wasn't involved in the project? How about your boss?

If you're working on something sensitive, take a few basic precautions. Don't leave important papers lying around. Lock up your desk and file cabinets before you leave for the night. Don't talk about the specifics of your work outside your team. (You can tell your significant other only if he or she doesn't pose a security risk.) Don't take out sensitive material in public—sensitive means anything that a competitor or journalist might find interesting. Be mindful of what you say over the phone, and be extra careful when sending faxes, e-mail, and voice messages: They can very easily end up in the wrong hands.

13

WORKING WITH CLIENTS

ABOUT WORKING WITH CLIENT TEAMS

It goes without saying that without clients there would be no McKinsey. They pay the (enormous) bills that keep the Firm going. It is not, therefore, surprising that McKinsey-ites are always told to put the client first. Hamish McDermott remarked that there was one true hierarchy at McKinsey: client, firm, you (in descending order).

In this chapter, we will cover the two different aspects of working with clients the McKinsey way. We will start with techniques to get the most out of a client team, the people from the client organization who work with McKinsey to reach a solution; we'll also look at ways to keep a client team from doing more harm than good. We will then move on to managing the client—in McKinsey's case, the senior people at the client organization who had called in the Firm to begin with. You will learn how to keep your clients engaged and supportive of your efforts and also how to make sure your solution actually gets implemented rather than gathering dust on a high shelf.

For some readers, the issue of client teams may seem remote. After all, if you are not a consultant, when will you actually have to deal with client teams? The answer is sooner than you might think. As a problem solver in a large organization, you may find yourself working with a team from, say, another business unit. Or you may be working on a joint venture with a team from an entirely different organization. In that case, you will, I hope, find the discussion of client teams as useful as the discussion of managing your client.

KEEP THE CLIENT TEAM ON YOUR SIDE

When you're working with a client team, you and the team have to work together or you won't work at all. Make sure that members of the client team understand why their efforts are important to you and beneficial for them.

The first thing to do when working with a client team is get them on your side. Make sure that they want to help you. At McKinsey, we learned that the key to keeping the client teams on our side was to turn their goals into our goals. They have to remember that if their mission fails, the McKinsey mission fails and if the McKinsey mission fails, their mission fails.

Members of the client team must also realize that working with McKinsey will be a positive experience for them. They must be made to understand that, at a minimum, they'll learn things that they would never otherwise know and that will help them in their careers. They'll also have a chance to make real change happen in their organization—a rare experience in most people's working lives.

For example, when I was working on a reorganization project for a Wall Street broker, my team worked with a client team made up of people from the IT department. One particular member of the client team, whom I'll call Morty, was a mainframe computer programmer, and looked the part. He stood about five and a half feet tall, in his business shoes, wore thick glasses and a suit that never quite fit; he lived with his parents in Brooklyn. Morty didn't really want to be on the client team; he had far too much "real" work to do.

Then I took Morty with me on a few interviews. He got to meet senior people in his organization: bankers, brokers and traders—the people at the front end of the business. He got to ask them questions and find out what they thought his department was supposed to be doing. Morty learned how to apply his own skills to solve problems he would not usually see in his day-to-day work. He also became noticeably more confident and outspoken during meetings as the study progressed. Working with McKinsey was an eye-opener for Morty, and he loved it (especially since he didn't have to write the interview notes; that job was left to me).

I'll close this section with a final note on the subject, and an apparent contradiction of something I wrote earlier (see "A Little Team Bonding Goes a Long Way" in Chapter 5). Team-bonding activities really add value when working with client teams. Since the client team is not bound by the same shared experiences as the McKinsey team, a little social interaction between the two can make working together a lot easier. A trip to the ballpark or dinner at a good restaurant (when people put away their "office faces") can help the members of each team realize that the others are real people too.

HOW TO DEAL WITH "LIABILITY" CLIENT TEAM MEMBERS

You may find that not everyone on the client team has the same abilities or goals as you do. Get "liability" members off the client team if you can; otherwise, work around them.

There are two kinds of "liability" members on a client team: the merely useless and the actively hostile. Ideally, neither type is on your team. If your career is typical, you'll probably get both.

On an engagement for a large New York bank, my team worked with a client team staffed with senior managers from various departments within the client organization: lending, investing, back office, and so on. Our member from the back office was a man I'll call Hank.

Hank was, shall we say, a diamond in the rough. He stood 6'4" tall and looked like a former football player who had let himself go—which, in fact, he was. His ties never matched his shirts and he invariably had food stains on his suit coat. Also, Hank knew his area of the bank inside and out and was probably as smart as any member of the McKinsey team.

Hank didn't want to work with McKinsey. He thought that the Firm peddled an expensive line of baloney to credulous clients and left the employees to clean up afterward He didn't want to be on the client team—he had real work to do. Still, his boss had assigned him to the team, so he showed up every day, and stubbornly refused to contribute. In short, Hank was useless.

How do you handle a Hank, or someone who is just too dumb or incompetent to do the work required of him? As a first (and easiest) tactic, you can try to trade the liability out of your team and get somebody better.

Trading doesn't always work, however; there might be no one better available and you're stuck with your own Hank. In that case, you have to deal with Hank. Work around him. Give him a discrete section of the work that he can do; make sure it is neither critical to the project nor impossible for anyone else on the team to do. You'll have to rely on the other members of the team pick up the slack.

For all his faults, Hank was better than Carlos. A superslick operator (BA, Oxford; MBA, Harvard) from Argentina, Carlos was the leader of the client team and our main liaison with the most senior management at the client. He was also a saboteur. Carlos had the patronage of a board-level faction within the client company that did not want McKinsey there; these board members felt they knew which direction McKinsey would recommend and they didn't like it.

Carlos subtly but actively prevented us from getting our job done. He sent us down blind alleys; he bad-mouthed us to the board behind our backs; he sabotaged us during presentations. We quickly realized that Carlos was not our friend.

Handling a Carlos, or any hostile client team member, is trickier than dealing with a Hank. Again, the best tactic is to trade the saboteur out of your team, but that's usually not feasible. If you have a Carlos on board, it's because someone powerful in the organization wants him there. The next best solution is to work around spies and saboteurs. Make use of their talents where you can and keep sensitive information out of their hands when possible. If you know who is behind the spy, find out what the ring leader's agenda is—maybe you can use that to your advantage when it comes time to sell your solution.

In our case, we had to leave Carlos to our ED, who had the political skill and muscle to handle him. Even then, Carlos remained a thorn in our side throughout the engagement.

Liability clients needn't be a disaster. Sometimes, you can even polish the rough diamonds. In Hank's case, after several weeks of working together, we managed to bond him to the team and got him to understand and, at least partially, buy into the McKinsey way of problem solving. In the end, he did contribute to our solution.

ENGAGE THE CLIENT IN THE PROCESS

If the client doesn't support you, your project will stall. Keep your clients engaged by keeping them involved.

To succeed as a management consultant or a business troubleshooter you must keep your client—be it your boss or the management of an organization that has hired you from the outside—engaged in the problem-solving process. Being engaged in the process means supporting your efforts, providing resources as needed, and caring about the outcome. With engagement thus defined, it is hard to imagine how any project could succeed without an engaged client.

The first step in keeping your clients engaged is to understand their agenda. Clients will support you only if they think your efforts contribute to their interests. Remember that their interests may change over time. Frequent contact and regular updates—even if it's just by memo—will help you keep in touch with your clients and keep your projects "top of mind" for them. Get on a client's calendar up front. Schedule progress meetings with tentative topics; if you need to reschedule, do it later.

Early "wins" (see "Pluck the Low-Hanging Fruit" in Chapter 3) will generate enthusiasm for your project—the bigger, the better. They give your clients something to sink their teeth into and make them feel included in the problem-solving process. The long-run returns on your work will be much greater if your clients feel that they were involved in reaching the solution and that they understood it, rather than being handed the solution neatly wrapped and tied with pink ribbon.

This brings us to one of the ironies of consulting. If you are an outside consultant, you will never get credit for your best work. If your solution is truly effective, the client organization will claim it for its own. Suzanne Tosini saw that firsthand as an associate at McKinsey:

> I developed a huge cashflow model that the client was going to use to evaluate real estate acquisitions. I had spent months on this project; it had been a Herculean effort. The client team members did some work on it, but essentially it was my model. When the time came to roll out the model, at a training program for the senior people in the acquisitions department, the client team members got up and talked about the model that *they* developed. I was sitting in the back and I thought, "Hey, that's my model." But then I realized that it was much better for them to think that it was theirs. It was not McKinsey's model, it was not Suzanne's model—it was their model.

> In truth, that's not such a bad thing.

GET BUY-IN THROUGHOUT THE ORGANIZATION

If your solution is to have a lasting impact on your client, you have to get support for it at all levels of the organization.

If you come up with a brilliant solution, structure it logically, and present it to your client with clarity and precision, then your job is done and you can go home, right? Wrong! If you want to create real change that has lasting impact, you must get acceptance for your solution from everyone in the organization that it affects.

For instance, suppose you tell your board of directors that they can boost widget profitability by reorganizing the widget sales force and streamlining the widget production process. Your argument is compelling; the board ratifies your suggestion; champagne corks pop and cigars ignite. One slight hitch remains: What do the sales force and the production-line workers think about all this? If they don't like your ideas, if they put up a fight, then your solution will not be implemented. It will end up on the great remainder shelf of business, right next to the Betamax.

To avoid this dire fate, you must sell your solution to every level of the organization, from the board on down. After you've presented to the board, present to middle-level managers. They will probably have day-to-day responsibility for implementing, so let them know what's going on. Don't neglect the people on the line, either. The changes you recommend may have the greatest effect on them, so their buy-in is vital to a successful implementation. Finally, serial presentations give the junior members of your team a good opportunity to hone their presentation skills.

Tailor your approach to your audience. Don't make the same presentation to, say, the fleet drivers as you would to the CEO. At the same time, respect your audience. Explain what is being done and why. Show people the entire picture. Let them know how their jobs fit into the organization as a whole. They're not stupid; they'll understand. Treat them with respect (remember, a lot of the time they don't get any) and they will respond positively most of the time.

BE RIGOROUS ABOUT IMPLEMENTATION

Making change happen takes a lot of work. Be rigorous and thorough. Make sure someone takes responsibility for getting the job done.

Implementing recommendations for change is a big subject. Whole books can be (and have been) written on it. I will limit myself here to explaining a few ground rules that McKinsey consultants have learned for implementing change.

To implement major change, you must operate according to a plan. Your implementation plan should be specific about what will happen and when—at the lowest possible level of detail. Don't just write:

We must reorganize the widget sales force.

Instead, write:

We must reorganize the widget sales force.

- Hold training sessions for all sales regions (Start: March 1. Responsibility: Tom.)

- Reallocate sales staff to new sales teams by customer type. (Start: March 15. Responsibility: Dick.)
- Take new sales teams to call on top 20 customers. (Start: April 1. Responsibility: Harriet.)

One former EM gave a no-holds-barred recipe for a successful implementation plan:

State what needs to be done, and when it needs to be done by, at such a level of detail and clarity that a fool can understand it.

Enough said.

Make specific people responsible for implementing the solution. Be careful about whom you pick. Make sure people have the skills necessary to get the job done. Enforce your deadlines and don't allow exceptions unless absolutely necessary.

The right point person can make implementation a very smooth process. If that person is not going to be you, make sure you pick someone who can "kick butt and take names." At one McKinsey client, an international bank, the managers chose a rather frightening fellow named Lothar to implement a major change program in their back-office processing. Lothar, who looked and sounded a bit like Arnold Schwarzenegger, had a very simple technique for getting the job done. Using the detailed McKinsey implementation plan, he assigned specific tasks to members of his team. Every two weeks the team would meet, and anybody who had not accomplished his or her tasks for the period had to explain the failure to the entire group. After the first meeting, when a few of the team members had undergone a grilling from Lothar, no one ever missed a deadline.

When, after a few months, the McKinsey EM rang Lothar for an update, he replied, "Everyone talks about how tough it is to implement. Seems pretty easy to me."

SURVIVING
AT
McKINSEY

In Part Four, you will learn a few tricks for surviving not just at McKinsey, but in any high-pressure organization. Whether you're trying to maintain your sanity while traveling for weeks at a time, trying to climb the greasy pole to success in your organization, or just trying to have a life while working 100 hours per week, there's something in Part Four that will help. As a bonus, I'll also shed a little light on the McKinsey recruiting process and even give a few tips for those of you who would like to try to join the Firm yourselves.

Contrary to what you might imagine after reading this far, there is more to life at McKinsey than work. Then again, there's not all that much more, which is why Part Four is so short.

14

FIND YOUR OWN MENTOR

Take advantage of others' experience if you can. Find someone senior in your organization to be your mentor.

As Tarzan once remarked, it's a jungle out there. To make your way through the corporate rain forest, it helps to have a guide, someone more experienced than you who can show you the hidden tracks and steer you clear of the quicksand. These days, the fashionable word for such a guide is *mentor*.

McKinsey maintains a comprehensive system of mentoring for its client service staff. Every consultant, from analyst to director,* is assigned a mentor to monitor and guide his or her career through the Firm. On the face of it, this sounds like a wonderful idea; it certainly seemed that way to me when, as an MBA, I was considering whether to join McKinsey's New York office.

As with so many wonderful ideas, the execution left a lot to be desired. I was assigned a mentor within my first week in the office, a very nice thirty-something partner. He bought me lunch at a trendy Italian eatery where supermodels popped in to nibble on arugula leaves. We talked about working at the Firm and how best to climb its greasy pole to success; it was a pleasant and informative 45 minutes. I saw him once after that. Within about six months, he transferred to Mexico to open a new office for the Firm south of the border.

After that, I got lost in the shuffle for several months. Eventually I was reassigned to another mentor. Although he had a good reputation as a mentor, I was one of 9 or 10 "mentees" that he had, and I got very little out of the relationship beyond the pro forma dissection of my performance reviews.

So, was I cast adrift in the Sea of McKinsey without a guide? Hardly. I did what most McKinsey-ites do when they want to succeed in the Firm: I hitched my wagon to a star. I did most of my work with one ED, the same ED who recruited me into the Firm.

---

*Actually, only the newer directors have mentors. In the case of the most senior directors, there is no one in the Firm to guide them. Rumors that certain senior DCSs have a direct videoconferencing line to a Higher Power can be safely dismissed.

We had a good relationship—call it chemistry. When I needed advice I couldn't get elsewhere, I went to him. He tried to get me assigned to his teams on studies where I had expertise. I was confident that, as long as I performed well for him, he would be in my corner when it came to assignments, reviews, and promotions.

My experience was typical of most McKinsey-ites. How much you benefited from your official mentor was pretty much a matter of luck. If you wanted guidance, you had to go out and get it.

I believe that's a lesson that applies in almost any large organization. Find someone senior to you whose abilities and opinion you respect; seek out the mentor's advice. Many people like to give advice and are happy to dispense it when asked. Of course, it helps if you get along well too. Work with the mentor, if possible, and learn all you can. Don't go to the well too often, however; you don't want to become a pest.

Whatever setup your organization has, make sure you find your own mentor. Having a guide you trust and respect will help you make it through your own corporate jungle.

15

SURVIVING ON THE ROAD

Traveling across the country (or the globe) can take a lot out of you. Making travel an adventure will lighten your load. So will proper planning and a good attitude.

Although working at McKinsey offers many advantages—good pay, interesting work, high-caliber colleagues—the working conditions can be grueling. On top of the long hours, which routinely include all-nighters, many McKinsey consultants spend most of their time on the road, away from home, family, and friends.

Sometimes business travel for the Firm can be fun: a week in London or Paris, and why not take the weekend skiing in the Alps? Just as often, however, working out of town only adds to the grind. There is nothing quite so mind-numbing, as one former EM noted, as the "If it's Tuesday, this must be Davenport" cross-country trips a consultant has to make when visiting all of, say, a manufacturing company's many plants across America. Even worse, you can find yourself commuting 1000 miles every Monday morning (or Sunday night) to some far-flung client, as happened to Hamish McDermott, who spent six long, cold months in Detroit working for one of the big car makers. That kind of travel takes a toll on your health, your relationships, and your sanity.*

McKinsey-ites have developed a number of ways to cope with the rigors of travel. They all agree on the importance of maintaining a proper attitude. Abe Bleiberg says:

> Try to look on business travel as an adventure. Even if I'm stuck in Flint, Michigan for three months over the winter, at least I can tell my grandchildren, "I survived a winter in Flint." Not everyone can say that.

Jason Klein adds:

> Act like a tourist. Make the most of where you are. If you're doing a project in Northern California and you're a golfer,

---

*On a personal note, I was a rare exception in that I spent only one night away from home while working for clients. Most of my clients were New York–based financial firms, so my commute meant getting on the subway to Wall Street. Because of this, I was regarded by my far-flung associate "classmates" with a certain amount of jealousy; on the other hand, I missed out on all those frequent-flyer miles.

take an afternoon and play Pebble Beach. You can keep your nose to the grindstone for only so long.

Remember that travel is an opportunity to do things outside your normal realm of experience. Here's Abe Bleiberg again:

Traveling as much as I did for McKinsey enabled me to meet people whom I would never otherwise have met. For instance, I once worked on a project where, in one meeting, people sat around a table trying to market toilet tissue. Never in a million years would I have ever been involved in selling toilet paper! It's not something I'd want to dedicate my life to, but that's part of the fun of working at the Firm.

Another key to surviving on the road: proper planning. If possible, schedule your time at the client to make sure you are at home on Fridays or Mondays. Pack light; learn what you need to have with you on the road, rather than what you think you need. If you can help it, fly with hand luggage only; just don't assume the airline will let you take that extra carry-on bag. If you're going to be in one place for a long time, find out if the hotel has a room where you can store your extra bags when you leave for the weekend—and make sure it's not the employee smoking room (as Adam Gold learned the hard way!). Find a reliable cab company. If you're renting a car, make sure you have clear and accurate directions to your destination. Otherwise, you might find yourself, as once happened to Hamish McDermott, coming off the interstate and onto the meanest of Detroit's mean streets with no on-ramp in sight (that's the sort of adventure you can do without).

Don't let the travel and the work become all-consuming, especially if you're out of town for a long time. Find a way to entertain yourself outside of work. Find colleagues, client team members, or maybe old friends from business school or college to have dinner with and catch a show or a ball game. At the very least, when you get back to the hotel do something before you go to sleep—whether it's working out, reading, or just watching television. Don't let being on the road become an uninterrupted cycle of working, eating and sleeping.

For one final survival tip I am indebted to Eric Hartz, now president of Security First Network Bank. He says:

> Treat everyone with tremendous respect. Sometimes McKinsey people can be demanding and impatient; then they fail to understand why they don't get what they want. Some of my colleagues were amazed at how I would get upgraded, or would get a bag on after the plane was full—things like that. Flight attendants, concierges, assistants at clients—these people have more authority than you realize and want to help those who show respect for them. It also keeps your stress level down—it's easier to be friendly than frustrated—so it's a win/win.

> That's possibly the best advice in this book.

16

TAKE THESE THREE THINGS WITH YOU WHEREVER YOU GO

Narrow your traveling needs down to the very few things you must have with you when you leave. Here are a few (mostly serious) ideas.

Anybody who travels frequently, whether for business or for pleasure, knows the three things you always take with you when traveling abroad, the famous PTM: passport, tickets, money. Whenever I travel on business, I always make sure I have three additional things with me: a copy of my itinerary, a list of the names and numbers of everyone I'm going to see, and a good book. Since, as I've said before, things at McKinsey usually come in threes, I asked the former McKinsey-ites I interviewed what three things they always have with them when they travel.

Here are some of the answers grouped by category (after all, this is a McKinsey list), along with explanatory notes, where appropriate.

Clothing
- An extra shirt or blouse
- Spare ties for the men
- Spare pair of comfortable flat shoes for the women
- Casual clothes
- Workout clothes ("It's easy to let your fitness slide when you're on the road.")
- A cashmere sweater for keeping warm and comfy on overnight flights.

Tools
- A writing pad
- A pad of graph paper (for hand-drawing charts)
- A copy of whatever you sent to the client
- An HP 12C calculator ("Better than a Swiss Army knife, although not quite as impressive on a date.")

Personal Care Items
- A toothbrush
- A shaving kit for the men

- A mini-makeup kit for the women
- Antacid tablets
- A bottle of Tylenol
- A *big* bottle of Tylenol

Things to Keep You Organized and in Touch
- A personal organizer
- Credit cards ("I keep them in a separate wallet.")
- The OAG™ (or other airline time table)
- A cell phone ("If I forget anything, I can just have it faxed.")
- Directions to the client (so you don't end up in the wrong part of Detroit)

Diversions
- A good book
- Press clippings to read on the plane
- Books on tape, especially if your travel includes long stretches of driving
- Video games on a laptop computer

The prize for the oddest answer has to go to a former McKinsey-ite from the Düsseldorf office who listed Coca-Cola. ("I traveled quite a bit in Eastern Europe. I can now drink Coke warm, cold, or hot without blinking.") Perhaps that belongs under personal care.

If these answers have a common theme, it's "be prepared." Make sure you're never caught short without something you really need. That being the case, the prize for the best three items goes to a former associate in the Washington, DC office (who justifiably wishes to remain anonymous). Our hero spent much of his time consulting in Brazil, where the weather, among other things, is unpredictable. This would-be Boy Scout's three indispensable items: an umbrella, sunglasses, and a box of condoms.

17

A GOOD ASSISTANT IS A LIFELINE

Call the position secretary, administrative assistant, or whatever. The person who takes your messages; keeps your schedule; does your typing, duplicating, and filing; and performs a dozen other office tasks is an exceptionally valuable resource. Treat your secretary well.

In McKinsey's New York office, the competition to hire good secretaries is as intense as that for top MBA graduates. Like any large organization, McKinsey would fall apart were it not for an efficient cadre of secretaries to handle the myriad administrative duties that the consultants are unavailable, unwilling or—frankly—unable to do. When consultants are on the road for much of the time, their secretaries are the lifeline that ties them to the rest of the Firm.

To attract the best, the Firm provides a real career path for secretaries. New recruits usually start out working with four or five associates. The good ones move on to work for SEMs; the best get claimed by partners and directors. Secretaries receive regular training, just like consultants, and they even get their own "retreat" every year. But there's more to the path than that. Many of the managers running the Firm's administrative and recruiting functions started out as secretaries; now they have positions of considerable power and responsibility. All this is designed to help McKinsey attract and retain the best secretaries, just as it seeks to attract and retain the best consultants.

A good secretary will perform numerous tasks that make a McKinsey consultant's life easier. These range from the obvious, such as typing, filing, and duplicating, to the not-so-obvious: filling out time sheets, paying credit card bills for consultants on long assignments, and sending flowers to significant others after yet another missed date. In fact, it is the less obvious tasks that really make a difference in a consultant's life. Most McKinsey-ites can do their own typing, many handle their own filing, and anyone can run the copier in a pinch. But knowing that there is someone "back home" whom you can trust to do those other, niggling little things that you would normally do if you were not 500 miles from your apartment for the next six months—that's going to make your life easier!

The alternative is pretty ugly. I saw a number of associates whose lives were a living hell because their secretaries were not up to scratch. Files got lost; faxes misdirected; messages appeared days after they were taken; clients were upset by poor telephone manners. One consultant, who was keeping two boyfriends in ignorance of each other, had her cover blown when her secretary, instead of saying she was in Houston all week, told boyfriend number 1 that she was at a lunch date with boyfriend number 2.

Associates at McKinsey have to take potluck with their secretaries. I was extremely lucky. Sandy, my secretary, was excellent from the start. Although I shared her with four other consultants, she always came through for me. I always gave her top marks in her evaluations (this made me nervous, because I was afraid a partner would poach her). I made a point of treating her well. This meant not just giving her flowers on Secretary's Day and something nice at Christmas; it meant giving her the respect she deserved in her job and making her job as easy to perform as possible.

I always tried to give my secretary clear instructions about what I wanted. I let her know where I was at all times during the day, so that she could reach me with important news or let clients and other consultants get in contact with me. Most important, I tried whenever possible to give her a chance to show initiative and make her own decisions: in putting together presentations, in running my schedule, and in acting as my interface with other consultants. This made ours a relationship from which we both benefited.

These days, of course, a lot of people do not have a full-time secretary. Maybe they just have a temp who comes in for a few hours a week, or a junior team member who gets stuck with the "grunt work." The principle remains: Treat them well, be clear about what you want, and give them room to grow. Sure, a temp will never rise in the corporate ranks, but you will still get better work out of him if you treat him with respect. The junior team member, on the other hand, will benefit immensely from a bit of careful nurturing. Take the time to train her well. Answering her questions and showing her the ropes will benefit you too.

18

RECRUITING McKINSEY STYLE: HOW TO DO IT

(AND HOW TO GET THROUGH IT)

McKinsey looks for specific attributes in a recruit. Here's how it finds them (and how you can show the Firm you have them).

One of McKinsey's goals, as listed in its mission statement, is "to build a firm that is able to attract, develop, excite, motivate, and retain exceptional people." The first stage in reaching that objective is recruiting the best possible candidates to join the Firm. As I've written elsewhere, McKinsey tries to skim off the cream, the elite of the elite at the top business schools, as well as law schools and economics and finance graduate programs. The Firm also goes out of its way to recruit "nontraditional" candidates from outside the realms of business academia: doctors, scientists, and politicians, among others.

Because the Firm takes recruiting so seriously, it commits serious resources to it—probably more, proportionately, than any other business organization. Every top business school, for instance, has its own team of McKinsey consultants assigned to it, complete with its own charge code for expenses. The expenses can add up too—sending four consultants from New York to Philadelphia, putting them up for five days at the best hotel in town, and taking out dozens of MBAs to fancy restaurants doesn't come cheap. Furthermore, the EM on the team makes recruiting a full-time commitment; at McKinsey's hourly rate, that represents a very large opportunity cost!

Even on a small scale, McKinsey doesn't pinch pennies. When Kristin Asleson took a highly courted JD-MBA out to lunch in New York, she took her to Le Cirque. Ivana Trump held court at a rear corner table. Walter Cronkite walked in. They nodded to each other. As Kristin recalls, "We both thought that was pretty cool."

With all this heavy weaponry, the Firm hunts first and foremost for analytical ability. As one former recruiter told me:

> I always looked for analytical thinkers, people who could
> break apart problems into their components. I wanted evi-

dence that they knew how to structure problems. I also looked for business judgment, the sense that the person knew the implications of his solutions. That's why I always used cases.

Cases are the weapon of choice in a McKinsey interview. They range from the prosaic—stripped-down versions of actual McKinsey cases—to the whimsical or even weird. Examples: "How many gas stations are there in the United States?" "Why are manhole covers round?"*

In a case interview, the interviewer wants to see how well the interviewee can think about a problem, rather than how correctly she answers it. As with most business problems, there is no one true answer. Rather, succeeding in a case interview requires breaking the problem into its component pieces, asking relevant questions, and making reasonable assumptions when necessary.

For instance, when figuring out the number of gas stations in the United States, you might start by asking how many cars there are in the country. The interviewer might tell you the number, or might say, "I don't know. You tell me." Well, you say to yourself, the population of the US is about 275 million. If the average household size (including singles) is, you guess, 2.5 people, than your trusty calculator** tells you that yields 110 million households. The reviewer nods in agreement. You recall hearing somewhere that the average household has 1.8 cars (or was that children?), so the United States must have 198 million cars. Now, if you can only figure out how

---

*When I was joining the Firm, one of my interviewers posed this challenge: "You've just been appointed special assistant to the Mayor of New York City. He wants to know how to make New York a better place. What do you tell him?" Being a native Bostonian, I could have said a lot of things (first of all, get rid of the Yankees and the Mets), but I concentrated on breaking the problem into its components. It worked.

**You never know when you might need your calculator! (See Chapter 16.)

many gas stations it takes to serve 198 million cars, you'll have the problem solved. What matters is not the numbers, but the method you use to reach them. When I was asked this question in an interview, I was off by a factor of 3, as the interviewer later told me, but it didn't matter for the purpose of testing my analytical ability.

There's more to the successful would-be McKinsey-ite than just analytical ability, however. McKinsey consultants work in teams, so personality counts too. As Abe Bleiberg put it:

> I assumed that most of the people who made it into the interview process were smart enough to work at the Firm. So I tried to answer the question: Did I really want to work with this person? Quite often, I rejected superintelligent, nasty people. One of the great joys for me was saying, "He's incredibly brilliant, and I wouldn't have him on my team for a million bucks."

Beyond a candidate's fit with the interviewer, there is also a candidate's fit with the Firm. To discover that, the interviewer has to get beyond the résumé and penetrate the polish. Given how slick many candidates are, the process can be tough.

For instance, Hamish McDermott met with one would-be McKinsey-ite from Harvard Business School. Hamish tried the typical opening interview gambit: "So, tell me a bit about yourself." Harvard Man proceeded to give a very structured, prepared, and long spiel listing all his strengths, virtues, and life experiences. Knowing that he was hearing a script, Hamish interrupted him with a question. "How would you characterize your analytical abilities?" he asked. Not wishing to break the flow of his monologue, Harvard Man replied, "I'll get back to that question in 10 minutes." As Hamish recalls, "That was not the response I was looking for." Oddly enough, Harvard Man did not get an offer to join the Firm.

No doubt, many of you want to know how to get a job at McKinsey. The answer is simple: Be of above average intelligence, possess a record of academic achievement at a good college and a top business school, show evidence of achievement in all previous jobs, and demonstrate extraordinary analytical ability. Simple to say, but not simple to do.

If you manage to clear all those hurdles, the key to your joining the Firm may be the case interview. I've already talked about cases, but I'll leave you with the best description of how to handle a case, courtesy of Jason Klein:

> I always asked the same case. I wasn't looking for a particular answer, but I wanted to see how people dealt with a complex problem in which a lot of information gets thrown at them at once. Some people froze; others just dug deeper and deeper. They were the people I recommended.

19

IF YOU WANT A LIFE, LAY DOWN SOME RULES

When you work 80 hours or more per week, after eating, sleeping, and (you hope) personal hygiene, there's not much time left over for anything else. If you want a life, you have to do a little advance work.

One especially bittersweet memory of my time at the Firm comes from a study I did for a Wall Street investment bank. My girlfriend (now my wife) worked as a portfolio strategist in the same building as my client, and she had a schedule just as punishing as mine. Many times during the five months of that study we shared a cab ride home—at 2 a.m.!

When I asked former McKinsey-ites how they left room for a social life, many of them replied that they didn't. As one of them told me, "I didn't do a good job of it because I didn't make enough rules. I was too afraid of jeopardizing my career." The lesson he learned (if only in hindsight) was that if you want a life when you work crazy hours, then you have to lay down some rules.

Hours of discussion with former McKinsey-ites have yielded three rules for a better life while at the Firm.

- **Make one day a week off-limits.** Pick a day—most people take Saturday or Sunday—and tell your boss (and yourself) that you never work on that day unless it's an absolute emergency. Most bosses (at least in my experience) will respect that most of the time. Make sure that you respect it too. Spend that day with your friends, your family, or just the Sunday papers. Keep your mind off work and relax a bit.

- **Don't take work home.** Keep work and home separate. If you need to stay at the office for another hour, that's better than coming home and ignoring your kids because you still have work to do. Home should be a place where you can be yourself.

- **Plan ahead.** If you travel during the workweek this is the most important rule. Don't come back from the airport on a Friday night and expect to find stuff to do over the weekend. When you're out of town, you're out of sight and out of mind, especially when you're single. If you want to do anything more than curl up with a good book, then you have to arrange things in advance.

Rules offer the great advantage of letting everyone know what to expect—your boss, your significant other, your kids, and you. Of course, it can sometimes be difficult to stick to even these very basic rules. When your priorities are "client, Firm, you," sometimes you have to let your life take a backseat to your career. That leads to my final rule:

- When all else fails, have a doorman. Then, at least, you'll come home to clean laundry.

PART FIVE

LIFE AFTER McKINSEY

As one former McKinsey-ite told me, leaving McKinsey is never a question of whether—it's a question of when. We used to say that the half-life of a class of new associates is about two years—by the end of that time, half will have left the Firm. That was true in my time there and still is today.

There *is* life after McKinsey, however. In fact, there may be more life, since you are unlikely to work the same hours at the same intensity in any other job. There is no doubt, however, that the vast majority of former McKinsey-ites land on their feet. A quick scan through the McKinsey Alumni Directory, which now contains some 5000 names, reveals any number of CEOs, CFOs, senior managers, professors, and politicians.

All those alumni carry with them memories of McKinsey, of lessons learned, of goals reached or missed. The Firm has left its mark on them as much as they left their marks on their clients. In these last few pages, I want to share some of those memories with you.

20
THE MOST VALUABLE LESSON

*Everyone who enters McKinsey leaves it
with a slightly different impression.
Although most former McKinsey-ites have
decidedly mixed views of the Firm, all would
say they learned important lessons there.*

In writing this book, I had two goals. The first was to transmit some of the skills and techniques that make McKinsey and McKinsey-ites so successful at what they do. The second goal was to convey to the outsider some idea of what it's like to work at McKinsey and with McKinsey people. By the time you've come this far in the book, I hope that I have succeeded in both.

As we reach the final pages, I wanted to share with you the answers to a question that I asked of every former McKinsey-ite I communicated with: "What was the most valuable lesson you learned at the Firm?" Some of the answers involve material you've already seen, at some length, in this book. Others describe lessons that cannot be taught—only learned. Here, in their own words, are the most valuable lessons learned by a baker's dozen of former McKinsey-ites:

> Preserve your integrity at all times. You will encounter any number of gray areas in business life—always take the high road. Do *The Wall Street Journal* test. If you are comfortable with reading about your actions on the front page of the WSJ, then it's OK. If not, you are pushing the ethical envelope—don't.
>
> —Eric Hartz, Atlanta/DC/Paris offices, 1986–95;
> now president of Security First Network Bank, Atlanta

> Consulting is best thought of as a profession. Putting the client first is the key to successful client service; to do so, you must maintain your professional objectivity. It has allowed me to stand my ground when a client hasn't heard what he wants to hear, or to walk away when the client doesn't want to work with me, and has helped me focus on what truly drives value for my clients.
>
> —Jeff Sakaguchi, LA office, 1989–95;
> now an associate partner at Andersen Consulting

Focusing resources and eliminating hierarchy lead to superior decision making. The Firm's clients had a hard time doing either one when attempting major change.

—Former EM in the Cleveland office

Personally, the most valuable lesson I learned was humility. I joined McKinsey as a 24-year-old associate with a track record of uninterrupted success. For the first time, I was surrounded by people who were better prepared and more skilled than I was. Professionally, I learned to structure problems so that they can be solved. The Firm taught me that every problem has a solution; it may not be perfect, but it will allow me to take actions that are directionally correct.

—Wesley Sand, Chicago office, 1993–96

I can't point to any one thing. It has to do with problem solving—the idea that any problem, no matter how daunting, can be broken into its constituents and solved. The other thing is that there is nothing new under the sun. Whatever you're doing, someone else has done it before—find that person.

—Suzanne Tosini, New York and Caracas offices, 1990–95; now a senior manager at Freddie Mac

The one firm concept. No stars, just meritocracy. That culture is extremely strong within the Firm, and I think it can work in other organizations too. I'm implementing it in mine.

—Gresham Brebach, former DCS in the New York office; now president and CEO of Nextera Enterprises

Execution and implementation are the key. A blue book is just a blue book, unless you do something with it. Getting things done is the most important thing.

—Former EM in the New York office

I learned to value strongly honesty and integrity in business—this is something McKinsey inculcates in its people and insists upon.

—Hamish McDermott, New York office, 1990–94;
    now a senior manager in a Wall Street investment bank

Don't fear end products. They go a long way. Generate end products.

—Former associate in the New York office

When faced with an amorphous situation, apply structure to it.

—Kristin Asleson, New York office, 1990–93; now working in Silicon Valley

I think anything I say would be too cynical.

—Former associate in the London office

I would rather be surrounded by smart people than have a huge budget. Smart people will get you there faster.

—Former associate in the New York office

You may be asking yourself, with some justification, what my most valuable lesson was. I've had a lot of time to think about that one. Here it goes:

> Anything that gets in the way of efficient communication is anathema to a strong organization. Fuzzy thinking, obfuscatory jargon, impenetrable hierarchy, and playing the "yes-man" get in the way of adding value for customers or clients. Structured thinking, clear language, a meritocracy with the obligation to dissent, and professional objectivity allow an organization and its people to reach their maximum potential. Of course, McKinsey has its own word for this—it's called "professionalism."
>
> —Ethan M. Rasiel, New York office, 1989–92

21

MEMORIES OF McKINSEY

The Firm leaves its alumni with vivid memories. Here is a sampling.

I asked former McKinsey-ites not only for their most valuable lesson, but also for the thing they remember most about the Firm. Although this selection shows that McKinsey alumni took away many memories, the strongest ones had to do with the people that make the Firm what it is:

> What stays with me is the rigorous standard of information and analysis, the proving and double-proving of every recommendation, combined with the high standard of communication both to clients and within the Firm.
>
> —Former associate in the Boston and New York offices

> The thing I remember most is the very high performance standards and the relentless drive for excellence that you see among the people there. It's not something you will necessarily find outside the Firm. There's an attitude within the Firm that says, "If there's a problem, give us the resources and we'll solve it. We'll just go out and do it." Outside the Firm, you often run into the attitude that says, "It can't be done," and that's just not acceptable at McKinsey.
>
> —Jason E. Klein, New York office, 1989–93;
> now president of *Field & Stream/Outdoor Life* magazine

The thing that I remember most, that I enjoyed most, was the team problem solving. I enjoyed the power of thinking in a small group of very smart people.

—Abe Bleiberg, Washington, DC office, 1990–96; now a vice president at Goldman Sachs

Structure, structure, structure. MECE, MECE, MECE. Hypothesis-driven, hypothesis-driven, hypothesis-driven.

—Former associate in the Düsseldorf and San Francisco offices

I have incredibly fond memories of the people at the Firm. There is a density of high-quality, smart, motivated people that I haven't found anywhere else.

—Hamish McDermott

The caliber of the people McKinsey recruits and retains throughout the organization—and not just in the consulting function.

—Former associate in the New York office

The people. On average, they are smart and fun to be with.

—Former EM in the New York office

The average mental capacity of the staff, be it the newest associate or the most senior director, and the approachability of people within the Firm, regardless of hierarchy.

—Gresh Brebach

The collegiate atmosphere. The thing I miss most about McKinsey is the canteen, not so much because the food was good, but because you could always take time out for an interesting conversation.

—Former associate in the London office

The quality of the people. In the corporate world, the average-caliber employee is far below McKinsey's least intelligent.

—Wesley Sand

The people, the wide range of people one came in contact with, both at the Firm and at the clients. McKinsey consultants shared a dedication to client service and a concern for the needs of the client.

—Suzanne Tosini

One of the advantages of being an author is that, at least within the confines of your own work, you get to have the last word. Where possible, I have tried to illustrate the key points in this book with stories from my experiences and those of former McKinsey-ites. For my last story, I'm going to reach a bit farther back than that.

One day in ancient Israel, a Gentile came to the great rabbi Shammai and asked of him, "Teach me the Law while I stand on one foot." Although he was a great scholar, Shammai, was not known for his patience; he called the Gentile impudent and chased him away. The Gentile then took his question to Shammai's great scholastic rival, Rabbi Hillel. Without hesitation, Hillel motioned the man to stand one-legged. While the Gentile balanced in the rabbi's study, Hillel told him, "Do unto others as you would have others do unto you. The rest derives from that. Go and learn."

What does this story have to do with McKinsey and with your career or business at the turn of the millenium? I'm not Hillel by a long stretch and the McKinsey way is not by any means holy writ. Still, it contains an essential core. To wit: Fact-based, structured thinking combined with professional integrity will get you on the road to your business goals. The rest derives from that. Go and learn.

INDEX

A

Actionable recommendations,
   10–11
Administrative assistants, 153–155
Agenda(s):
   and client engagement, 133
   meeting, 121
Annual reports, 74–75
Anxiety, interviewee, 86–88
Approach, development of, 15–28
   with difficult problems, 24–28
   and identification of the
      problem, 15–16
   and initial hypothesis, 21–22
   tool kit for, 17–19
   and unique client characteristics,
      19–20, 22–24
Assertiveness, 69
Assistants, 153–155
Associates, McKinsey, 5
AT&T, 57

B

"Bellyaches up front" technique,
   100–101
Best practices, 75–76
Big picture, looking at the, 41–42
Bill Clinton approach, 64
Blue books, 34, 107, 172
Body language, 82
"Boiling the ocean," 32
Bonding, team, 61–62, 130

Boss:
   communicating with, 120
   enhancing image of, 67–68
   of interviewee, 83
Brainstorming, 93–101
   exercises for, 100–101
   preparation for, 95–96
   "rules" for, 96–100
Brevity (of messages), 122
Business travel (see Travel)
Buy-in, getting, 134–135

C

Case interviews, 159–161
Chain of command, McKinsey,
   65–66
Charts, 113–118
   daily, 37–38
   simplicity in, 114–116
   waterfall, 117–118
Client teams, 127–137
   engagement of, 133–134
   getting buy-in from, 134–135
   goals of, 129–130
   "liability" members of, 130–132
   thoroughness with, 136–137
Client(s):
   "prewiring," 109–111
   as priority, 170
   promises made to, 53–55
   unique characteristics of,
      19–20, 22–24

Clothing, travel, 150
Columbo tactic, 85–86
Communication(s):
    importance of efficient, 173
    internal, 119–125
Confidentiality, 123–125
Credibility, maintaining, 40–41
Credibility gap, 5
Culture, McKinsey, 114, 171

D
Daily charts, 37–38
Data, researching, 71–76
Datastream, 72
DCS (director of client services), 53*n*
Difficult interviews, 88–90
Difficult problems, solving, 24–28
Director of client services (DCS),
    53*n*
Dun & Bradstreet, 72

E
EDs (*see* Engagement directors)
80/20 rule, 30–31
Elevator test, 34–35
EMs (*see* Engagement managers)
End products, 172
Engagement directors (EDs), 42*n*
    as bosses, 67
    brainstorming by, 93
    choosing of associates by, 60
    in McKinsey hierarchy, 65–66
    as mentors, 142–143
    and presentation changes, 108
    structuring of engagement by,
        53–54
    team selection by, 59
Engagement managers (EMs), 2*n*
    as bosses, 67
    brainstorming by, 93
    choosing of associates by, 60
    in McKinsey hierarchy, 65–66
    and presentation changes, 108
    and recruiting, 158

Engagement managers (EMs)
    (*Cont.*):
    and team morale, 63, 64
    team selection by, 59
Engagement(s):
    first day of, 4
    structuring, 53–54
    team, 133–134
Entertainment, 147–148

F
Fact packs, 93
Facts:
    arriving at solution from, 24–25
    importance of, 4–5
Failure, 41
Flipchart exercise, 100
Flipcharts, 99–100
Forces at Work, 18

G
Grunt, McKinsey, 81
Gut instincts, 4, 5

H
Hierarchy, 65–69
    aggressive strategy for managing,
        68–69
    eliminating, 171
    and pleasing the boss, 67–68
High-pressure organizations,
        surviving at (*see* Surviving
        at McKinsey)
Hillel, Rabbi, 177–178
"Hitting singles," 39–41
Home, separating work and, 164
Honesty, 42, 172

I
"I don't know," saying, 42–43
"I have no idea," refusing to
        accept, 44–45

IH (*see* Initial hypothesis)
Implementation, 136–137, 172
In Search of Excellence (Peters and Waterman), 51
Informal marketing, 50–52
Initial hypothesis (IH), 8–13, 21–22
   defining, 9–10
   generating, 10–12
   testing, 13
Integrity, professional, 42, 172
Internal communications, 119–125
   and confidentiality, 123–125
   and flow of information, 120–121
   keys to effective, 122–123
Internet, 72
Interviews, 77–92
   anxiety of interviewees in, 86–88
   case, 159–161
   difficult, 88–90
   indirect approach to, 84–85
   listening and guiding during, 81–83
   preparing for, 79–80
   thank-you notes as follow-up to, 91–92
   tips for successful, 83–86
Issue list, 6–8
Issue tree, 12

J
Japanese (language), 81*n*

K
Key drivers, 10–11, 33–34

L
Leaders, meeting, 121
"Leads," chart, 115
Leakage, 21
Lessons of working at McKinsey, 169–173
Lexis/Nexis, 72
"Liability" team members, 130–132

Listening (during interviews), 81–83, 83–84
Low-hanging fruit, plucking the, 36–37, 133

M
Marketing, informal, 50–52
The McKinsey Quarterly, 51
MECE, 6–8
Meetings, 121
Memories of McKinsey, 175–178
Mentor, finding a, 141–143
Messages, 121–123
"Mix," team, 59–60
Morale, team, 62–64
Mushroom Method, 120

O
"Off-limits" day, 164
Ohmae, Kenichi, 51
Open-ended questions, asking, 84
Other Issues, 8
Outliers, 75

P
Paraphrasing, 84
Partners (*see* Engagement directors)
PD (*see* Practice development)
PDNet, 72–73, 93
Perfectionism, 107–108
Performance standards, 175
Personal care items (for travel), 150–151
Peters, Tom, 51
Plucking the low-hanging fruit, 36–37, 133
Politics, working through, 28
Post-it exercise, 100
Practice development (PD), 68–69
Preparation:
   for brainstorming, 95–96
   of clients, 109–111

Preparation: (*Cont.*):
   for interviewing, 79–80
Presentations, 105–111
   perfectionist approach to,
      107–108
   preparing client for, 109–111
   structure of, 106–107
"Prewiring" clients, 109–111
Problem solving, 2, 171
Procter & Gamble, 35
Professional integrity, 42, 172
Professional objectivity,
      maintaining, 170
Professionalism, 173
Profit and loss statement,
      re-creating competitor's,
      44–45
Promises to client, making, 53–55
"Pulling rank," 89

Q

Questions:
   in brainstorming sessions, 98
   open-ended, 84

R

Random encounters, 121
Recommendations, actionable,
      10–11
Recruiting, 157–161
   allocating resources for, 158
   and analytical ability of
      candidates, 158–159
   and "fit" of candidates, 160
Redefining the problem, 27
Reinventing the wheel, 17–19,
      72–74
Research, 71–76
   "smart," 72–74
   tips for conducting, 74–76
Resources, focusing, 171
Respect:
   for teammates, 62, 64
   treating others with, 148

S

Sandbaggers, 90
Say It With Charts (Gene Zelazny),
   113
Secretaries, 153–155
"Selling" the study, 49–55, 104–137
   with charts, 113–118
   and flow of communications,
      119–125
   and informal marketing, 50–52
   with presentations, 105–111
   and promises to client, 53–55
   and working with client teams,
      127–137
SEMs (*see* Senior engagement
      managers)
Senior engagement managers
      (SEMs), 4*n*, 97, 154
Silence, 82–83
Simplicity:
   in charts, 114–116
   and key drivers, 33
Social life, rules for maintaining,
      163–165
Square Law of Computation, 33
Structure:
   applying, 172
   of engagements, 53–54
   of messages, 123
   of presentations, 106–107
Surviving at McKinsey, 140–165
   business travel, 145–151
   and importance of a good
      secretary, 153–155
   mentor, finding a, 141–143
   recruiting, 157–161
   rules for, 163–165

T

"Tag-teams," 83
Teams, 13
   assessing morale of, 62–64
   bonding within, 61–62, 130
   client, 127–137
   communicating with, 121

Teams (*Cont.*):
    engagement of, 133–134
    getting buy-in from, 134–135
    goals of, 129–130
    "liability" members of,
        130–132
    McKinsey, 57–64
    "mix" of, 59–60
    thoroughness with, 136–137
Thank-you notes, 91–92
Thoroughness, 136–137
Three (as magic number), 3*n*
Tool kit, 17–19
Tools, travel, 150
Trade publications, 10
Travel, 145–151
    entertainment during, 147–148
    items for, 149–151
    maintaining proper attitude for,
        146–147
    planning for, 147, 151,
        164–165

Travel (*Cont.*):
    treating others with respect
        during, 148
Tweaking, 28

U
Unique client characteristics,
    19–20, 22–24
Unrealistic expectations, creating,
    40

W
The Wall Street Journal test, 170
Waterfall chart, 117–118
Waterman, Robert H. Jr., 51
White boards, 99

Z
Zelazny, Gene, 113

ABOUT THE AUTHOR

Ethan M. Rasiel joined McKinsey & Company's New York office in 1989 and worked there until 1992. While at "the Firm," his clients included major companies in the finance, telecommunications, computing, and consumer goods sectors. He has also worked as an investment banker and an equity fund manager. He has a bachelor's degree from Princeton and an MBA from Wharton. He now lives with his wife and family in Chapel Hill, North Carolina.